OFFICE HACKS

How to work less and achieve more

The perfect gift for anyone working in a (home) office

James. O. King

To Isabel and Amadea, my current and former colleagues, and to all those who helped create this book.

Thank you!

Foreword

Dear Reader,

You spend approximately 8 hours at the office – five days a week. That's over 1,800 hours a year, or the equivalent of watching 900 movies. That's also too much time spent working without using "office hacks."

The "office hacks" contained in this book a collection of highly useful and practical tips on how to make your daily office work easier and accelerate your career. You will learn how to get your boss to appreciate you more, be more popular at the office, ensure that your "ass is covered" in case of trouble and much more.

Whether you are an office "old-timer" or a "new-timer" in an internship or entry position, this book was written for you. I guarantee that this book will pay for itself by saving you countless hours and improving your salary prospects.

In writing this book, I systematically documented my own "office hacks" gleaned from nearly a decade in corporate offices of both small and large companies. I also reached out to grizzled "office veterans" worldwide and asked them for their tips and tricks. Finally, I asked readers for their feedback, including regarding whether to include some commonsense hacks. This curated collection of "office hacks" is the result.

When reading this book, think about which hacks are most relevant and beneficial to your specific situation. Not all workplaces are the same, so take the time to consider which hacks would be most effective at helping you achieve your goals. What may be helpful to a controller may not be relevant to a secretary or marketer – and vice-versa.

To make the most of this book, write down which hacks are most useful to you and start implementing them at work. Don't try to change everything at once – start slowly!

For simplicity and brevity, I have often used male pronouns in this book. This is not meant to exclude women, without whom offices worldwide would be much worse off. I have also refrained from explaining technological or software hacks in all their detail. This was done intentionally since new updates or technological developments would render the hack outdated within a short amount of time. To make it easier for you, I have pointed out when you should use Google or another search engine to find the most up-to-date instructions for a hack.

If you have any suggestions or feedback, I would love to hear from you! Reach out via James.O.King@outlook.com.

More content can be found at www.winnerhacks.com

Enjoy reading and enjoy hacking your workday!

Table of Contents

Getting a good job	1
Your first days at the office	16
Doing work as efficiently as possible	30
IT office hacks	60
Getting a good routine	72
Getting your boss to promote you	102
Covering Your Ass (CYA)	114
Optimizing your workspace & staying healthy	123
Unethical hacks	132
Leadership hacks	147
General pointers & miscellaneous hacks	160
Leaving your job	173
About the author	179

Getting a good job

Your job location and what company or organization you work for are two factors that have some of the biggest impacts on your personal and professional life. That is why the very first chapter of this book is dedicated to helping you make that all-important decision and figure out how to successfully get hired at your ideal company. The tips and techniques listed below are based on input from headhunters, HR-employees and hiring managers – so start hacking your way to your dream job!

1. Find out what you want to do first.

This point cannot be overstressed. If you're only doing a job for the money, you probably won't be successful or be doing it for very long.
Reflect on your strengths – are you a good orator, a numbers guy, or an efficient coordinator? Having a job that plays to your strengths makes your life a lot easier.
Think about which person in your family or circle of friends has a job that you'd like to have. Or just think about people whom you've interacted with in general and thought to yourself, "I wish I had his/her job."
Another good approach here is to think about what job you would still do even if it were really underpaid or you suddenly won the lottery.

2. Search for insights into the job before applying.

Search engines like Google are your best friend when you want to find out about more a new job. Say you're interested in consulting. Search for "best aspects of consulting," "worst aspects of consulting," and "what to do after consulting." You may also want to consider similar search-terms like "an insider account of...," "forum for...," "the truth about...," and "lies about...." Social media sites like Facebook and Reddit usually also have pages dedicated to the job or industry you're looking into.
Hint: Get in touch with the people who wrote about or provided information on the job or industry you're researching. They will typically answer more specific questions you have or can even help you get a job.

3. Talk to people in the field before applying.

If you know someone in the field you are interested in, then reach out and talk to them about what their job is <u>really</u> like. If you don't know anyone, ask around to find out if someone you know knows someone (who knows someone etc.).
Hint: Rather than just writing an email with questions, invite that person out for a coffee or meal. It is a nice gesture and the relaxed atmosphere will allow for a more open and insightful conversation.

***

4. Research what happens with employees.

Using LinkedIn or Google, try to find out more about employees in the company you are applying to. Have long-time employees been promoted to CEO/CFO/CIO? What companies did past employees switch to? How many are part of industry associations or are mentioned in trade magazines or the media? These are some factors that can help you decide whether or not to apply to a particular company.

5. Use anonymous employer-rating sites.

Glassdoor.com, kununu.com, reviews.greatplacetowork.com and indeed.com are just a few of the online employer-rating sites available. You can find out salary ranges, benefits and easily compare different companies in the field with one another.
Hint: Some companies try to tweak their ratings by getting employees to write positive reviews – be suspicious if a large number of 5-star reviews are written within days of one another.

6. Try to get referred.

A lot of companies offer their employees rewards if they can refer proficient individuals for a vacancy. Smaller companies are happy to give candidates recommended by current employees a chance, without them having to go through the cumbersome application process. If you know someone at the company you want to apply to, ask them if they can refer you or help you get a foot in the door. A personal referral usually puts you at an advantage over other applicants.
Hint: Even if you don't know someone personally, you can always search on LinkedIn for an employee and write to them. If an employee you contacted on LinkedIn wants to refer you, take the time to talk to them once or twice before providing your CV. You need to know the person who referred you (at least a little bit), in case you are asked about them in your interview.

7. Use headhunters.

A headhunter's job consists of matching people to vacancies at companies. Headhunters take most of the administrative hassle and stress out of job hunting. The only thing you have to do is provide them with a bit of starting information (what you want to do, where you want to work, what your salary expectations are, etc.) and then turn up to the interviews with your potential new employer.

Finding headhunters is as easy as Googling the search terms "headhunter + [your target industry]." If in doubt, go for the larger headhunters in your country, as their size is usually a result of their successful track record in matching people to vacancies. Larger headhunters also have a larger number of vacancies, increasing the likelihood that you'll find your perfect match.

Hint: You can still reach out to headhunters if you are just starting your career. Companies also recruit junior positions and headhunters are happy to help their customers – no matter the seniority of the vacancy. Be aware that if you want to work for a prestigious company, their strict recruiting standards (grades, target universities, extracurriculars) still apply – no headhunter can change that.

Hint: Even if you aren't interested in the positions the headhunters are offering you, you should save their contact details. Having the emails and phone numbers of fifty industry headhunters will make finding a new job a lot easier.

Hint: There are unprofessional headhunters out there who want you to sign a contract as fast as possible so that they can get paid. You can usually distinguish how serious a headhunter is by the amount of time they spend getting to know you and which

companies they are filling vacancies for (good companies are picky about which headhunters they work with).
Hint: Tell your headhunter to keep your job search confidential. You don't want your current employer to find out that you are looking for a new job.

8. Experience > academic records.

If your grades aren't high enough to get into your dream company, join another company in the same industry to gain experience. During this time, network with people from your dream company as much as you can. Then switch after having built up at least a year of relevant experience. If you highlight your newly acquired skills in application and know people in your dream company, your grades won't be as relevant.

9. Exploit HR application software.

Many companies use software to filter out applications before someone from HR has a chance to examine them. To exploit these software systems, simply use the same keywords and terms as are listed in the job description. The HR software will rate you as a candidate with more relevant experience and give you a higher score.

For example, if the position requires "quantitative analysis skills" then your application should contain these very words or slight variations thereof ("quantitatively analyzed data").

Hint: Don't bend the truth as you can be fired for lying on your application. Just rephrase your application to match the job description so that the HR software scores you higher.

10. Don't copy your application.

An increasing number of companies use HR software that identifies plagiarism in your CV or cover letter. If the software says you plagiarized, your application will be filtered out automatically. You can always use sample CVs and cover letters for reference, but never copy and paste.
Here is how to get the best input from others' documents while avoiding the risk of plagiarism:

- Search the web or ask friends for good samples of cover letters or CVs (aim for at least 10 examples)

- Read the cover letters or CVs you collected and write down phrases and layouts you would like to use for your own application on a <u>separate</u>, blank sheet of paper. Writing in pen or pencil reduces the temptation to simply ctrl+C and ctrl+V.

- Using only the sheet of paper with your handwritten notes as reference, draft your own cover letter or CV. Your handwritten notes will include a mix of ideas and phrases that reduce the risk of HR software flagging your application as plagiarized.

Hint: Have a few friends (especially those who work in HR or are responsible for hiring) give you feedback on your application to improve its quality. Multiple reviews or iterations will result in wording changes which further reduce the chances of plagiarism.

11. Invest time for important applications.

Landing a job at an awesome company greatly increases your chances of working for other awesome companies — kind of like a chain reaction. Go that extra mile to land a job at a good company and it will pay dividends for many years to come. This advice to invest quality time to complete important applications was repeated by a lot of the office veterans interviewed for this book. Joining the right company at the right time can mean the difference between billionaire CEO and lower management pawn.

Hint: Tips and tricks on how to write applications and ace interviews would be a whole book in itself. Here are a few of my favorite pieces of advice:

- Think of your application as an advertisement – use it to make yourself as attractive and relevant as possible.

- Make your cover letter one page. Ensure your CV is no longer than two pages. Be aware that in addition to content, your application will also be judged on spelling and formatting. So, spend some time making your CV look visually appealing.

- Pick up on points from the job description and convey how you have or can demonstrate those qualities. Once you have written your cover letter and CV, use a green highlighter and highlight every point from the job description you covered

- Write using short sentences, action verbs and aim for the present tense. Use "I lead software sales" instead of "I am overseeing the sale of software systems". Try to avoid using qualifying or moderating words like "can" instead of "will," "would" or "could". This may seem just like a diction choice or semantic change, but it automatically makes the reader see you as a more attractive candidate. Think about it, would you buy the toothpaste that "can" or "could" give you whiter teeth? Or would you buy the one that whitens your teeth?

- Adopt expressions and terminology from your target company's latest press releases. Press releases are usually reviewed by a lot of employees (including senior leadership). You should also read interviews or watch speeches given by your target company's senior leadership. This will make your application sound like leadership material and provide you with good talking points for your interview.

- Take out anything that doesn't directly relate to the role you're applying for or improve your standing. That extracurricular award ten years ago? Not relevant. The less clutter the HR employee or your potential boss has to read through, the better.

- Save or send your application as a PDF and make sure it has a sensible file name (e.g. lastname_application.pdf).

12. Think about your salary expectations.

Unfortunately, it is still frowned upon to ask potential employers about what salary they are willing to pay you.
A better solution is to ask what the salary range for that position is – companies typically agree on a salary range for each job before publishing a vacancy. If their maximum salary is too low, don't hesitate to say so. Just be professional about it, i.e. say "the range you mentioned would leave me worse off financially" and not just "that's not enough."
If you are switching positions, adding at least 5-10% to your current salary is a good rule of thumb.

Hint: Some negotiation books tell you to start with a very high salary figure in order to "anchor" the other person. However, Pokering too high can lead to you being disqualified or considered to be too expensive.

Hint: If you Google "salary [your job title]" you can find forums or other platforms where typical salary ranges are discussed. Depending on the size of the company you are joining, you can also add your future company's name to the above search terms.

Hint: No salary is set in stone. If you make a good case as to what you are bringing to the company and the value you are adding, you should ask for a higher salary.

Hint: If you can, write "negotiable" when asked for your expected salary. This will reduce the chance that your application is thrown out because of too high or too low expectations. Be sure to research what a reasonable salary for your position is, so that you know what to ask for in the interview or once you get an offer.

13. Call HR & ask some easy questions before applying.

This "hack" is based on the expectation of HR employees treating your application favorably. It is much harder for an HR employee to bin your CV when they can still remember your voice and the positive interpersonal connection you built up during the call.

As an added bonus, you will also know what person from HR you can directly speak to about the status of your application or to follow up if you get rejected.

This "hack" is all about following the right sequence. It goes as follows:

- Call the company recruiting hotline or HR contact person listed in the job description.

- Say you have some questions and ask to be connected with the HR employee responsible for the specific vacancy you are applying to.

- Once connected to the relevant HR person, introduce yourself with your name and 2-3 points which highlight how interested or qualified you are for the position (e.g. "Hi, this is John Smith. I'm in my last year of business administration and was really impressed with the work [insert company name here] did on [insert something you found on their website]. As someone who loves [insert topic related to vacancy] and with relevant experience in [insert topic related to field], I was wondering if I could ask you some questions to see whether I would be a good match for your vacancy"). Not only does this short introduction enable you to showcase your experience and interest, it also makes your call stand out compared to other applicants).

- Prepare 2-3 relevant but easily answerable questions (in advance!) and ask them. Being able to answer your questions immediately puts the HR employee in a positive mood since they feel knowledgeable and useful. Sample questions may be "How large is the team?", "What backgrounds do other employees typically have?", "Would my certification in [industry] be relevant for the vacancy?", "It says that three years of experience are required, could I still apply despite only having two and a half years of experience?", etc. Avoid questions which require the HR employee to get back to you at a later time.

- Thank the HR employee for having answered your questions and indicate that, based on the positive answers to your questions, you will be sending in your application later that day (or the next day / upcoming weekend). Be specific about when you are going to send your application so that your application stands out even more (the HR employee will be expecting it).

Hint: The above phone call only works if you are able to maintain a cheerful conversation. Awkward pauses, off-color jokes or strange questions may result in your application going straight to the shredder.

Hint: Humans are uniquely equipped to identify a person's mood based on their voice. Watch a funny YouTube video or read a comic in order to be in a good mood before calling. You can also try some deep-breathing exercises to release stress and put yourself at ease. A happy, joyful, unstressed voice will put the HR employee at ease and in a good mood too.

Hint: You should have a nearly final version of your application ready before your HR call. That way, you can easily submit your application on time. If you obtain some new insights from your HR call, tweak your application before submitting it.

Hint: You can also use your HR call to make your cover letter introduction easier and more personal. Say you talked to Mrs. Crassus from HR. Then your cover letter could start off with "Dear Mrs. Crassus, thank you for the informative call yesterday. Based on your insights regarding the team's background and the role's technological focus, my attached CV should be of high interest… etc." Addressing your CV to "Mrs. Crassus" instead of "to whom it may concern" also increases your chances of success.

14. Stand tall or pace when calling.

Whether it's a first-round phone interview or a follow-up call, standing up straight when talking helps. Standing reduces the pressure on your diaphragm, adding depth and strength to your voice. The physical act of standing also has psychological effects, making you sound more confident and likely to adopt a fluent pattern of conversation (think about it – we do most of our talking when standing or walking).

15. Do practice interviews.

Interviews are like everything else – practice makes perfect. Send out applications to other companies in the same industry at least four weeks before applying to your dream companies. That way, you have some practice interviews under your belt and can perform much better when it comes to the interviews you really care about.
Hint: Research the most commonly asked questions for your target industry or company, and then practice until you have perfected answering them. Think of further questions that would stress you ("Why do you have a gap in your CV?") and practice answering them. Practicing the most commonly asked questions and your personal "stress questions" will eliminate a huge portion of the interview stress.
Hint: You can find other people to practice interviews with by Googling relevant websites or forums (e.g. "interview practice partner automotive engineer"). Thanks to Skype, WhatsApp and Zoom, practicing with strangers has never been easier. Practicing with other applicants is a lot better than practicing with your family or friends. You get a direct insight into how other applicants are presenting themselves and what kind of

competition you could be facing. Unlike family or friends, other applicants will also be more direct in their feedback. As an added benefit, practicing with others will provide you with a valuable network within your industry.

Hint: If you do practice with other applicants, don't make it all about you. Make an effort to really help the other person and provide them with useful feedback. Be punctual for practice sessions. Stay in touch after you land your job. The world is a small place – you don't want to have made a bad impression on your former practice buddies who are now working in the same industry as you.

16. Always think aloud in interviews.

Make it easy for your interviewer to help you. Talk your interviewer through your thinking process, so that he or she can give you hints or nudges. Try to structure your thoughts as much as possible and proceed chronologically – e.g., "First, I would think about what costs arise. When looking at costs, I would look at fixed and variable costs. For fixed costs, I would..."

Thinking aloud also enables you to get some of the "points" even though your final answer may be wrong. Very often, interviewers care more about the thought process behind your answer than the actual answer you provide.

Hint: If you don't know the answer to a question, just say so. In order not to seem incompetent, you can add where you would look to get an answer – e.g. "I don't know how insulin is refined. If I had to find out, I would Google it as a first step and then read relevant studies and reports. I would also ask colleagues and reach out to universities, pharmaceutical companies and industry associations as well."

***

17. Follow up – even if you didn't make the cut.

If you were rejected, ask for the reasons why. Receiving feedback on why you didn't make it this time will increase your chances of a successful application in the future.

If you want, you can reiterate that you are very interested in working for the company that rejected you and ask when you could apply again. When you do apply a second or third time, you may have a better chance of success by being remembered as an applicant who is highly motivated to work at that specific company.

If you did an interview with potential colleagues (i.e., not HR but the people you would have been working with) add them on LinkedIn or send them an email. Thank them for their time, tell them that you enjoyed the interview and ask if it would be OK to keep in touch since you are still interested in their company or industry. A good relationship with past interview partners is very beneficial as the world is surprisingly small and you might run into your ex-interview partners sometime in your career. You can, of course, also ask past interview partners for feedback on your application or tips regarding the interview if you choose to apply a second or third time.

***

18. Keep your job description after joining.

Save a copy of the job you applied to. If you are doing more complex and demanding tasks, you can refer to this job description when asking for a raise or promotion.

If you want to leave your company, you can also use the job description as a checklist to ensure you included all your responsibilities and qualifications on your CV.

***

19. Keep looking.

If you aren't happy at your job, you should continue looking for a better one. Switching to another company is also a good idea if you know that a promotion isn't going to be happening anytime soon (due to no vacancies, bureaucratic processes, office politics, etc.).

YOUR FIRST DAYS AT THE OFFICE

First impressions count – especially when you're starting a new job or joining a new team. Your first few weeks are all about getting to know people and getting a feel for who does what and why. Building your own reputation and knowing the right people will make your working life much easier, so start using the "hacks" listed below during those crucial first few weeks.

20. Pretend you are still being interviewed.

Congratulations on successfully interviewing and getting the job! Just remember that you haven't yet made yourself valuable to your new company. Have a mindset that you need to prove that you deserve to be hired – at the very least during your probationary period. Having this mindset will make you work harder and smarter as well as make a good, long-lasting first impression.

✱ ✱ ✱

21. Ask the "W" questions.

When given a task, ask the "W" questions to help you organize and prioritize your workload:

- <u>Who</u> is the final recipient of your work and who else will it be shared with? (internal stakeholders vs. customers or senior management vs. engineers)

- <u>What</u> should the final result look like? (PPTX vs. DOCX vs. XLSX)
- <u>When</u> does the task need to be done? (discuss deadlines for drafts and final versions)
- <u>Who</u> are the people relevant to this task? (colleagues, external partners, or individuals on the customer side)
- <u>Where</u> can I find relevant input / data / slides? (avoid reinventing the wheel)
- <u>Why</u> is this important? (this helps you get an idea of where your task fits into the bigger picture and gain a deeper understanding of the subject)

22. Ask for feedback often.

During those precious first days and weeks, you should be asking your direct boss many questions. What did you do well? In what areas could you improve? Questions like these show your commitment and will help create a solid first impression.
Hint: Be sure to ask your manager what things you did well on. This forces your boss to think about positive feedback for you – feedback you can use at the end of your probationary period or promotion discussions.

23. Office decorations are an excellent icebreaker.

When meeting new colleagues, make it a point to notice the pictures, plants, and other decorations on your co-workers' table. People generally love talking about themselves and will be happy to tell you the stories that the rest of the office has already heard. Focusing on their decoration will help you start conversations and build a personal connection very early on – something which bland questions about the weather or traffic won't do. Noting colleagues' decorations will also help you to remember their names (Susan, the mom of triplets; Frank, the cactus collector, etc.)

★★★

24. Listen closely and pay attention.

Spend the first few weeks getting a feel for your office. Listen to what others are explicitly or implicitly saying, and look out for unspoken rules as well as established group dynamics. Pay attention to how things are done and who is responsible for what.
Ask as many questions as you can during your first few weeks. Being new gives you a carte blanche to ask about anything and everything.
Don't try to change things from day one; there are probably good reasons for why things are the way they are.

★★★

25. Follow up quickly after meeting new people.

If you've just met some new people at a convention or large meeting, a short email or LinkedIn contact request will help them remember who you are and provide them with your contact details. The email in question doesn't have to be much more than "Really liked your opinion on the new marketing concept. Great meeting you."

★★★

26. Build real relationships with customers ASAP.

Customers are the lifeblood of your employer. If you succeed with customers, your company will reward you. Interpersonal relationships are vital for winning customer business, so get to know your customers on a personal level – not just as names, titles, and email addresses. Build up real relationships by talking about personal topics, going to lunch together, introducing them to other people in your network, sending birthday or Christmas wishes, or forwarding them news articles or new studies which they may find interesting.

Generally speaking, you want to make it as easy as possible for them to do business with you. Think about it: would you rather do business with someone whom you like, trust, and know, or someone who is impersonal, distant, and highly formal?

Hint: A real relationship with a customer can be a highly valuable source of information. Do you want to know whether a new product or service would be of interest to them? Do you want to be introduced to someone else within your customer's company that will provide you with an invaluable informal channel into their company? Did you lose some of their business and not know why? A good relationship means you can just call your customer and ask.

27. Use LinkedIn or similar social media.

During your first few days / weeks / months, you should add people you've met to your LinkedIn. That way, you have a backup solution in case you forget their name or what they look like. You can also read up on their professional backgrounds, which can make for good conversation topics or provide you with a more complete picture on their expertise or experience (i.e. what that person is good at).

***

28. Learn to ask for forgotten names gracefully.

While new at the office, you can ask for people's names multiple times without seeming like a forgetful idiot. After a certain point however, asking for names you've forgotten just becomes awkward. Some people take offense if you don't remember their name, so here are several "hacks" to find out names without directly asking:

- Discreetly ask someone else (the best way).
- Ask to see their business card and say you want to compare it to yours.
- Find your company organizational chart and use the process of elimination.
- Search for emails or mailing lists which you know they are on. You can also search for calendar invites or past meetings and deduce their names from the attendee list.
- Enter some relevant information into Google and look at the image search results until you find their face (e.g., university degree & year of graduation, sports club they are a member of, past company, current job title, etc.).
- Prompt an introduction between two colleagues. Imagine you're talking to Frank (the colleague whose name you know) when you bump into a colleague whose name you've forgotten. Just say: "Hey Frank, do you two know each other already?" Either Frank says "Yes, I already know Tim," or "No. Hi, I'm Frank. What's your name?" This also

works if you're part of a group meeting or lunch and prompt a short introduction of all participants.

- Ask if they've Googled their name to see if it means anything etymologically, what the geographic origins of their name is or whether someone else with the same name turns up prior to them in the search results. The unknown colleague will usually repeat their name when answering your question.

29. Find out how your performance is measured.

The sooner you know what really matters when negotiating salaries or promotions, the better. Take the initiative and ask your boss as well as colleagues about the concrete expectations for your job – i.e. how your performance is assessed. Knowing how your performance is measured during your first days will quickly help you prioritize which people and activities to focus on.

30. Keep an eye on desk traffic.

Look around your office and see who is always out to lunch with different people or has the highest number of people dropping by their desk. This person usually knows a lot of people in the office and can help you quickly find the right person or be a good source of information.

31. Have a candy dish.

Depending on your role in the office, you may want to get a small dish of candy and place it near the entrance or at the edge of your desk closest to visitors. Nearly everyone likes candy – you will be surprised at how often people will flock to your desk and socialize. This small dish of candy will pay for itself in terms of colleagues sharing the newest information, bonding or doing you a favor sometime down the road in reciprocity for your sugary generosity. Veteran office workers swear by this candy dish hack for good reason. Try it.

Hint: If you are a secretary or have a lot of physical customer or colleague interaction, then this hack is for you. Experiment with what candy or salted snack is most popular in your office.

Hint: Bring sweets or snacks from a different region or country if you come from there or spent your last holiday there. Having more exotic candy or snacks is a great ice-breaker.

Hint: If you want to put out candy, you had better do it from the first day. Suddenly starting after many years at the office just seems strange. If you do want to start all of a sudden, you should choose a holiday such as Easter, Christmas or Halloween and fill the dish with seasonal candies. After the holiday is over, just make your candy dish a permanent feature.

32. Make friends outside your department – especially HR.

Friends in other departments can save you hours and hours of work. Instead of waiting weeks on answers via the formal route, you can just make a short call or meet your friend for a quick coffee.

This is especially true for HR or controlling, so be sure to make friends there. Whenever promotions or layoffs are discussed, HR and controlling are always involved. Having a friend who speaks up for you or gives you a heads-up can make all the difference.

33. Make friends with the "non-office" people.

Use your first few weeks and months to make friends with as many of the secretaries and non-office people (cafeteria staff, janitors, etc.) as possible. They may just warn you when the boss is not in a good mood, save you the last bit of your favorite ice cream, or notify you if there are extra parking spaces available. They may also help you get appointments with the really important people in your company.

Being on a first-name basis and showing your appreciation with a few chocolates or flowers (e.g. on secretary's day or birthdays) goes a long way. You'll be surprised at how many amazing "non-office" people work in your company – and disappointed in how few of your office colleagues make the effort of getting to know them.

34. Make friends with the workers' council, industry association or union.

Depending on your country, workers' councils or unions may have more or less power. In any case, they typically know about developments or changes in your company or industry before you do. Getting a heads up before a planned organizational change or knowing about an upcoming strategy or C-level change can make all the difference to your career. Having friends there can also make you a valuable go-to source for news in your department.

Hint: You can always apply to become a member of the workers' council or union. These positions are usually protected by law and give you power as well as other perks. Be aware that such a position can also have downsides such as being blacklisted within your industry or passed over for promotions. Talk to past or current members of your workers' council or union about their experience first before applying.

35. Use lunches to build relationships.

While new at the office, you should always have at least two weeks of lunch or coffee dates scheduled in your calendar. Check if someone has a free slot in their calendar and send them an invitation saying you're new and would like to get to know them – you will almost always get a yes.

A good approach is to ask coworkers what the best coffee or lunch spots are and ask if they'd like to go sometime. Asking for their favorite place enables a more relaxed and intimate conversation as opposed to a boring canteen conversation.

Hint: If you're going to a coworker's favorite place and they can't come, ask them if they want to order some take-away for you to pick up. They will appreciate the offer and remember the nice gesture.

Hint: During your first few weeks, you should watch out not to ruin any longtime established lunch traditions. Employees who have been there for years may have established routines. Until you get a better feel of the unspoken traditions, ask questions like "What do you usually do for lunch?" or "Do you mind if I come along?" rather than "Let's do lunch tomorrow."

36. Read internal guidelines and policies.

After reaching a certain size, companies start codifying all of their rules. HR usually leaves it up to you to read these documents – you would be surprised at how many employees don't take full advantage of the valuable information contained therein.

Does your company offer free health checks every two years? Are you eligible for a company contribution to your private pension? Are there discounts available to you as an employee? Can you use your company laptop or mobile phone for private internet surfing?

How many warnings do you have to receive before you can be fired? What is considered overtime? How many days can you be absent without a doctor's note? What happens to your pension contributions if you leave the company? What is the maximum acceptable price for a hotel room? What are the criteria for expensing meals?

The answers to these questions and other similar ones are typically found in your company's guidelines and policies. You can only hack the rules to your advantage if you know them — so take the time to read them. If you feel treated unfairly and can point to a policy which supports your behavior, chances are that you will quickly win the argument.

Hint: Don't expect colleagues or HR to make you aware of all the perks and rights listed in your company policies — it is up to you. Knowing about policies also makes you a valuable source of knowledge for colleagues. Just be sure to tell colleagues to check the latest version as policies and guidelines are changing regularly and you don't want to be giving bad or outdated advice.

Hint: If you are in doubt regarding an ambivalently formulated policy, get written clarification so that you have "covered your ass." When asking for clarification concerning a policy, be sure to think about how to formulate your request to maximize the chances of a positive answer (i.e. "I would like to reward my team for their good work with a team event. What is the maximum cost I can incur to motivate my team?")

Hint: In some companies, you can become part of the team writing the policies and guidelines. Doing so can help you shape the rules to your benefit. A working mother did so and was able to include perks in the "maternal leave policy" which her male colleagues would not have thought of.

37. Find a mentor.

Most people love to help others and pass on their knowledge to someone younger or more junior. If you know someone at work who has had a really good career (i.e. been promoted quickly or is already high up in the corporate ladder), ask them to be your mentor. Just say that you're very impressed with their work and would like to have them as a mentor – it's that easy. You'll benefit from their tips and tricks as well as having an additional senior person who is watching out for you and your professional success.

Hint: Some companies have official programs where you can be matched with a mentor – use them. If your match is not up to par, ask someone to be your unofficial mentor. In order to increase the chances of them becoming your mentor, make your request a bit personal. Find something about your future mentor that you would like to learn ("I really liked the way you handled that sales presentation – would you mind mentoring me so I can learn from the best?"). Adjust how you ask and the thickness of your flattery depending on the personality of your potential mentor.

Hint: Set up regular lunches or similar meetings to keep on track of things – at least once a month. In the first few meetings, you should clarify what you're looking to achieve so that your mentor can decide on how best to help you. Mentioning that your meetings are completely confidential will help your mentor open up more and provide you with behind-the-scenes insights. A thank-you card or similar token of appreciation every so often goes a long way too.

Hint: Setting up the first lunch or meeting with your mentor is as simple as asking them in the hallway or giving them a short call – don't just send an email invitation. Say something along the lines of "Hi Laura, thanks again for agreeing to mentor me. It really means a lot to me. When could we have lunch together to get to know one another a little better?" Try to meet outside of work (i.e., don't have lunch in the cafeteria) – your mentor will speak more freely and on a more personal level with you. As a rule, you should pay for lunch. Your mentor will (consciously or subconsciously) feel indebted to you and want to pay you back. This concept of indebtedness and reciprocation is deeply rooted in our biology. Think about it – would companies really spend hundreds of billions of dollars on business lunches and dinners if there was no "return on investment"? Your mentor will also probably say "let me get the next one," (in which case you have already laid the groundwork for regular meetings).

Hint: Don't make meetings with your mentor all about yourself – keep the meetings somewhat balanced. Ask your mentor about their personal and business life. There may be some issues you can help your mentor with, especially since you (typically being younger than your mentor) will probably be better informed on current trends and technologies (see the "reverse mentoring" approach detailed below for more details) .

Hint: If you are young and want to build a relationship with the more senior leadership, join (or offer to set up) a "reverse mentoring" program. As a "reverse mentor," you provide your expertise on what your generation is doing and thinking, as well as on new technological trends. I can guarantee you that only a small percentage of Fortune 500 leaders know how TikTok, Tinder or Snapchat works – which makes your insights as a young person extremely valuable.

* * *

38. Find events and clubs near your workplace.

You spend so much of your life near the office; it can never hurt to know a few more people in the area. Find a sport or hobby you enjoy and see if there are any get-togethers nearby. Not only can you regularly get some perspective from people who don't work at your company, you can also leverage this new network and introduce colleagues from your office that may also share an interest in the same hobby or sport as you do.

* * *

39. Get a leather organizer and a nice pen.

Spend a bit of money to buy an organizer (also known as padfolio, portfolio or compendium) and a nice pen. You will look more professional. Even if you don't like them, think of them as props which boost your credibility. As one lawyer who interviewed for this book said, "Everything you say becomes a lot more credible after you elegantly uncap your expensive pen and open your expensive leather organizer at the start of a meeting."

* * *

40. Setup a good voicemail greeting.

A professional voicemail greeting makes a good impression on the caller and is not that common anymore. A good example of a voicemail greeting is "Hi you have reached [name] at [company].

Please leave your name, number and a short message after the beep. I will get back to you as soon as possible." Check with your company to see if they have a standardized script – larger corporations do.

Hint: When recording your voicemail greeting, do it while standing up to ensure your voice sounds steady and powerful. You should also be in a good mood when speaking so that your voicemail sounds cheerful.

41. Google ethnic names.

If you don't know a colleague and are unsure whether to address them as "Mr." or "Mrs.," you can search the name on Google and look at the image results. If there are a lot of men shown, you can be quite sure that the name belongs to a man. If you want to be really sure, ask a colleague you both have in common or try to find their LinkedIn profile.

42. Pay it back.

When someone new joins your office, offer to answer any questions they may have or help with names. Check in with them regularly to see how they're doing – this makes a world of difference to them.

DOING WORK AS EFFICIENTLY AS POSSIBLE

The overused phrase "don't work hard, work smart" exists for a reason. Work should be all about results – how you spend your time getting those results should be up to you. Here are a few hacks to help you prioritize your time, be more efficient in what you do, and avoid additional work.

43. Stop multitasking.

Studies on multitasking have proven that doing multiple things at once ends up costing you more time than it saves. It's virtually impossible for humans to focus on more than one thing at once and do them well. Our brains are biologically predisposed to switch between individual tasks quickly, pausing one and picking up the other.

To make matters worse, multitasking has a wide range of negative impacts on the human mind, from higher stress levels, to lowering your ability to memorize and concentrate.

If you do find yourself tempted to multitask, create a to-do list, do each task individually and tick it off. You'll work through your list far faster than by multitasking.

To stop multitasking, you must also avoid constantly checking your emails. Each email is a distraction that can set you off on a completely different tangent. Set yourself intervals of 30 minutes during which you don't check your inbox. Deactivating your email notifications or temporarily putting Outlook in offline mode are also good ideas.

***

44. Split your work into EoD, EoW & long-term.

Any work you do can be split into individual tasks you need to do by End of Day (EoD), End of Week (EoW) or long-term. Keeping such a simple system allows you to prioritize your time and quickly see whether you still have time left for any given day or week. It is also really nice to tick off things once you're done.
Hint: Write your EoD, EoW and long-term tasks on a whiteboard; it makes you look organized and lets your boss see all the tasks you're working on.
Hint: You can make the EoD list for the next day before leaving work. That way, you can spot potential challenges early on.

***

45. Do small things immediately.

If a new task can be completed within 5 minutes, do it immediately. If not, add it to your to do list, block some time to specifically work on it, and get back to whatever you were doing before. Preventing all those distracting 5-minute tasks from quickly piling up and occupying valuable brain capacity will make you more efficient.

***

46. Work in short bursts.

There is no conclusive figure as to how many minutes the average human can concentrate for. Some studies suggest that we start to lose focus after 10-20 minutes. Some studies say that we can concentrate for longer periods of time, while other studies say that in this digital age our attention span has shortened to less than 5 minutes.

Whatever the exact figure may be, it makes sense to work in short bursts.

One of the more popular methods is the Pomodoro Technique, which involves working in 25-minute sessions, followed by a five-minute break. Try it out and adjust the working session time to fit your personal ability to concentrate.

Hint: If your deadline allows, put your current piece of work aside and attack it again at a later time. Working on something else, taking a short break, or having a good night's sleep allows your subconscious to better reflect on your work and gives your brain a small respite. When you return to the work you put aside, you will be much more effective.

47. Make the first hour count.

Your first hour at work is usually the most productive – don't waste it. Use that first hour to work on your most challenging tasks and to think about problems which require creativity or are highly complex.

Avoid looking at your email inbox during that first hour – the world will keep on turning even if your emails remain unanswered a little longer. If you do feel the need to check your inbox, give yourself 5 minutes and ignore any email that is not essential.

Hint: Set yourself a daily meeting in Outlook to avoid others taking that precious first hour away from you.

48. Achieve one thing every day.

Before arriving at work, think about which single task would make your day a success if you were to complete it. Force yourself to complete the sentence "today would be a success if I finish…" with one realistic goal.

By setting yourself a realistic goal (and successfully completing it), you create a highly motivating psychological positive feedback loop. Over a work year, you will have achieved over 220 of your daily goals – which is a lot better than juggling too many tasks at once while not making real progress on any single one.

49. Set deadlines.

This is an underrated "hack" that borders on a superpower. Whenever you're working with other people, you can magically focus their efforts by setting a deadline. People will start prioritizing their work in order to meet the deadline you just set. If someone responds that they can't make your deadline, you can make use of three simple questions. Ask "what can you finish by then?", "how do you suggest we meet the deadline?" or "how much more time would you need?" These questions put the onus on the other person to come up with a solution.

Hint: The deadline does not have to be completely realistic. Humans are target-seeking and will strive to meet even a somewhat unrealistic date. Even if not all the work is completed by your deadline, your team will probably have made significant progress in a short time.

Hint: You can also provide deadlines which already contain buffers. If someone is unable to meet your deadline, you can use these buffers to easily give them more time without endangering

your real deadline. This can also make you look generous – just don't do it too often or your deadlines will lose their credibility.
Hint: Make sure that everyone involved knows about your deadline. The more prominent your deadline is, the more people will magically focus in order to meet it. A prominent deadline also negates any "I didn't know" excuses.

You can send reminders 1-2 days before your deadline to ensure that no one forgot about it. Another approach is to schedule a meeting on the day of your deadline to discuss the work that had to be done. This is very effective as the people you invited will want to be prepared for the meeting you scheduled.

Hint: You can also set deadlines for yourself. Setting yourself a deadline also works magic for your ability to focus and quickly finish tasks.

✶ ✶ ✶

50. Learn to say no.

You wouldn't guess it, but this is one of the most important hacks to have a good time at the office. Too often you feel compelled to say yes in order to avoid being labeled as unmotivated, lazy or not a team player. If you are already busy or simply don't want to do something, just say no.

Learning to say no doesn't mean categorically saying no to everything and everyone. It also doesn't mean that you will be considered lazy or unhelpful. It just means you prioritize your work. If you are unsure about whether to say "yes" to an additional assignment, ask your boss their opinion.

Saying yes to everything makes everyone unhappy. It makes you (and your family) unhappy since you must now cram even more work into your day. It makes your boss and your colleagues unhappy since you are not focused on your assignments or are missing deadlines due to juggling too many tasks at once. Committing to too many things also lowers the quality of your work. Saying "yes" to other assignments means saying "no" to time dedicated to proofreading or reviewing a document.

Hint: Pay attention to how often others say "no." This goes especially for managers, directors, and executives; these persons typically get to where they are by saying "no" often. You can also learn a lot by listening to <u>how</u> they say "no."

Hint: If someone pressures you to say "yes," you can always reply that you need to check with your boss first, or that you can only do it later (saying a really far-off date is just as good as saying no). You could also list all the things you are currently working on, or ask if they can't think of someone else who may be better suited or available. Most colleagues will get the hint and look for someone else.

Hint: Even if it is your boss asking you to do overtime and you feel like you shouldn't decline, don't say "Yes Sir, right away Sir." Instead, you can half-jokingly say, "just this once, and only because it's you" or "is there no other poor bastard you could find?" in order to make your boss aware that overtime is an exception and not the rule. If exceptions become the rule, sit down and have a serious discussion with your boss.

51. Be honest about your workload.

Don't fall into the trap of saying "it will take just a second" or "sure, I'll squeeze it in." Be honest and realistic about how busy you currently are.

If something is going to take 4 days to do, then give an estimate of at least 4 days. If something is urgent, don't be afraid to clearly communicate what other tasks and deadlines you need to shift in order to finish the new task.

When shifting tasks and deadlines, be sure to inform your boss and other affected persons immediately. Give them a chance to react and adjust their plans.

Hint: Always give a generous estimate as to when and how long it would take you to do any additional task. There is a scientifically proven "planning fallacy" effect which causes us to be overly optimistic regarding how long a task will take and therefore underestimate the time required. Overestimating the necessary time and effort counters this optimism bias. A generous estimate also increases your chances of looking good by finishing "ahead of schedule and under budget."

52. Write three questions for each meeting.

At the start of each workday, take a look at the meetings you're supposed to attend that day. Spend a few minutes to think of the three questions you would like to have answered in each meeting. This will help you focus on what your goals for each meeting are and help you answer the question of whether that meeting is worth attending at all. As a rule, if you can't come up with important questions you want answered within 30 seconds, it is a good sign you should not attend that meeting.

53. Prioritize – aggressively.

Since you won't live or work forever, you want to spend your time at the office doing things that are "high impact, low effort." For a manager, that could mean spending less time on tweaking a PowerPoint presentation and more time on coaching employees. For a project manager, that could mean spending less time adding the hundredth parameter to a business case and more time on perfecting the customer experience.

To find out what your "high impact, low effort" activities are, you want to draw the matrix shown below. On this matrix, plot all the different activities you <u>could</u> spend your time on. Effort (y-axis) is the total amount of time required and Impact (x-axis) is the overall benefit or value to your company. Once you have plotted all your activities, spend your work focusing on the activities in the <u>lower-right quadrant</u>. Having such a matrix can also be a very useful basis for talking to your boss about how you want to spend your time at work and what trainings you would like to take.

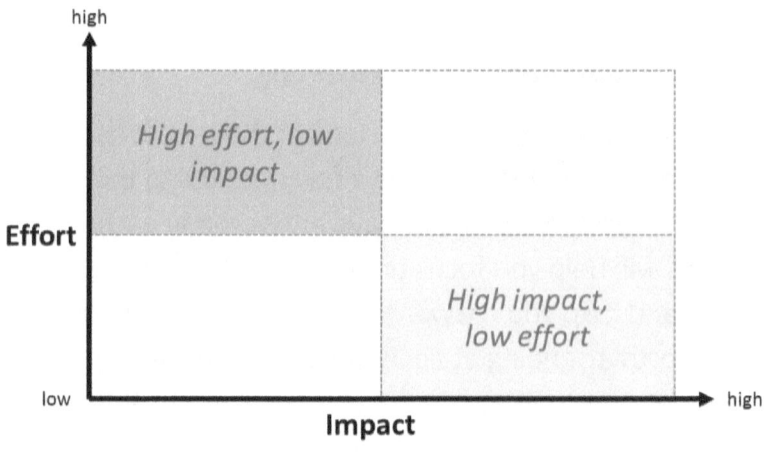

★★★

54. Take the initiative.

In offices, as in life, sometimes it is easier to ask for forgiveness than wait for permission. If you are confident that the potential positives of an action outweigh the potential negatives, take the initiative and do it. Just be sure your action can't lead to a catastrophic meltdown or viral "shitstorm."

This also goes for the everyday decisions. If you're in a group trying to find out where to eat for lunch, take the initiative and confidentially throw out a suggestion. The same goes for volunteering or throwing out ideas or questions in meetings – you don't always have to be right. Others will start to see you as assertive, which is a trait also associated with competency and leadership.

★★★

55. Test simply, fail fast.

This clichéd phrase can save you hundreds of days of work. To use it, just think of the simplest way to test whether an idea has merit or not. That way, you can quickly stop wasting your time on an idea that has no value – i.e., you can fail fast. Use this "test simply, fail fast" anytime you start working on a new idea or on an improvement to an existing product or service.

A few examples to illustrate this approach:

- Your boss thinks your company app needs a chat function. Instead of spending thousands of dollars and hundreds of hours programming it, just ask your app developer to add a fake "chat now" button. Whenever someone clicks this fake "chat now" button, they get the message "Thank you for your interest. We are currently testing the demand for a chat function." Record how many people used your app and how many clicked the "chat now" button. If there isn't enough demand, you just saved yourself (and your company) a huge amount of money and time.

- Your colleagues can't agree on what marketing slogan for a new product works best. Use the top three marketing suggestions and show them to 100 randomly selected potential customers each. By getting customer feedback at an early stage, you have potentially saved your company millions of ineffective marketing expenditure.

56. Learn to write effective emails.

Writing effective emails is an invaluable hack that will save you (and your recipients) hundreds of hours each year. Although there are entire books written on how to write emails, the most important rules are listed below:

- **Check if you really need an email in the first place**. If your email concerns a topic that is likely to require some back-and-forth, a short call or chat is more efficient.

- **Emails are forever!** Don't write anything in an email you wouldn't mind showing your boss or reading on a billboard by your office. Every email you send is recorded – so write every email as if it could be forwarded to your CEO.

- **Don't stretch the truth in an email**. Don't downplay a problem or deliberately leave out important details known to you. Best case, you look uninformed. Worst case, you get known for deliberately misrepresenting the truth and your reputation/trustworthiness suffers.

- **Don't write angry.** Even though it may feel therapeutic, an angry email will not get you far. You will probably anger your recipient and lose their support or goodwill. A better approach is to refocus the conversation on what needs to be done and casually name a superior in your reply. You can always talk to a friend and bitch about your frustrations. If you really want to write an angry email, then wait 24 hours before hitting "send" to see if it's still appropriate.

- **Think about what you need before starting**. This helps you be more precise about what input you need (and who to write). Structuring a problem also greatly increases the likelihood of a reply being useful.

- **Less is more.** The shorter and more precise the email, the better.

- **Choose a tone**. Write an informal email if you have a good relationship with the recipient as intimacy leads to favors. If you mean business, adopt a more formal tone. Choose between thanks/thank you, sorry/unfortunately, can you/could you please, see you soon/yours sincerely and so on.
  The maximum number of exclamation points in a business e-mail? One. Otherwise, you risk looking childish and unprofessional.

- **Be positive**. Try to phrase your email positively. Words like "agreed," "good point," "together," "useful," "will do my best," or "grateful" will psychologically help to win over your reader. Try to avoid conveying an accusatory tone or words with negative connotations such as "impossible" or "can't".

- **State your request in your email's subject line**. Always use a subject line that clearly states what you need and succinctly summarizes what your email is about. Compare "Summary of our meeting" to "Review needed by Friday noon – Minutes of Meeting with ABC Company on 30.06.2018."

- **Use "EOM" when a subject line is all you need**. If your email consists of only a few words, write those few words in the subject line and end with "EOM" (end of message). E.g. "Will be 10 minutes late. EOM," "Reminder: please send last sales report. EOM" or "Is our meeting with Katharina still happening at 13:00? EOM."

- **Use structure**. Use bullet points, paragraphs or bold headlines to give your email some structure. This makes it a lot easier for your recipient to understand your questions or requests. A simple structure may be along the lines of "problem," "context" or "status" and "alternatives" or "next steps."

- **Start by concisely explaining your reason for writing the email.** Establish the context early on so that your recipient can read the rest of your email with that context in mind. If someone told you to contact the person you're emailing, tell them who did and why. Don't build up to why you're sending an email – emails are not mystery novels.

- **Only include relevant content**. Avoid writing "see changes made on page 334 of the attached report." Take a screenshot of the relevant page or send only the relevant pages as an attachment.

- **Be as direct as possible**. Clearly state what you want the reader to do ("I need your signoff by Friday 12:00" or "Can you review the meeting minutes and send them out by tonight?"). Depending on your local culture, being too direct can be considered impolite.

- **Keep sentences simple**. Don't use complex, run-on sentences which your recipient has to read multiple times. Keep sentences simple and short.

- **Use numbered lists.** This helps the recipient address each point individually and quickly reference an individual point (e.g. "Question 14").

- **Highlight the ToDos.** Make what you need stand out clearly. Use bold, underlined or differently colored/highlighted text to make sure your reader knows what they should do. Include deadlines so that your recipient can prioritize what you are asking them for. If you expect questions, tell them when you can be reached by phone.

- **Say who needs to do what.** If your email has multiple recipients, write names next to the "to dos" or the content especially relevant to them. E.g., "@Sarah: See attached sales offer" or "@Andrew: Need an OK from legal by 18:00 today." Try to write this at the top of your email to enable each recipient to know what to focus on when reading the rest of your email.

- **Check the conversation history.** Emails are often forwarded without deleting the previous conversation history. Take the 10 seconds to check that you aren't accidentally sharing sensitive or personal information.

- **Proofread your email.** Focus on spelling, grammar and the understandability of your email. Pretend you are the recipient and are reading your email for the first time. Spelling mistakes or difficult-to-understand sentences distract the reader from the content of your email and damage your overall credibility.

- **Always include a signature.** Not only does it look professional, it also provides your recipient with your phone number.
- **Get feedback.** If writing an important email, ask a colleague to read it and give you feedback.
- **Mark emails as important only if they really are.** If you mark all of your emails as important, your recipients will start to ignore them.
- **CC or BCC.** If in doubt, err on the side of caution and put others on CC – if only to "cover your ass." Adding your boss or colleagues on CC gives your email more gravitas. Use BCC if you want to send one email to multiple recipients who don't/shouldn't know each other (e.g., a rejection email to multiple consultancies). Just send the email to yourself and BCC everyone else.
- **Fill in the "To:" field last.** When writing an email, leave the "to:" field empty until you have re-read your email and are ready to send. Alternatively, you can also add all recipients and then add a recipient called "STOP." Outlook will not send out the email unless this "STOP" recipient is removed.
- **Respond quickly.** People notice and reply to your emails quickly as well.

57. Planning & tracking progress is half of success.

You can read a lot of project management handbooks, but most of what makes a project succeed or fail is really down to planning and tracking progress correctly.

Hacks for **planning** (really invest time into this, ideally before or at the start of your project):

- Concretely define <u>what</u> your project wants to achieve (a.k.a. the project focus, scope, aims or objectives)
- Define <u>who</u> is responsible for what
- Outline the individual <u>activities</u> and results / deliverables required (ideally together with your team)
- Identify <u>what</u> other resources, people or input you need (this is especially important if you need key resources or people not readily available)
- Arrange the activities on a <u>timeline</u>, prioritize them and define milestones
- Give everyone the opportunity to provide <u>feedback</u> on your project plan
- Get everyone to <u>signoff</u> (commit) and then start the project
- Use your project plan to <u>communicate</u> (often!) with people and synchronize with them

Hacks for **tracking** progress (the more you communicate and coordinate, the better):

- Set up regular "checkpoint" or "status" meetings with your project team
- Have key people give a quick report on what they are working on and whether they are facing any problems (depending on the project complexity and company culture, this can be anything from a 10-minute daily standup to a 1-hour meeting with formal status reports)

- Keep an up-to-date list issues or problems mentioned to systematically solve them

- Set up a regular meeting with your boss and other key stakeholders to ensure you are both on the same page

- Don't be afraid to escalate problems if you can't easily solve them. Other people can only help your o your project <u>if</u> they know that something is going wrong.

Hint: If your company doesn't have any standard project management templates, you can always just Google search for templates. Typical search terms are "project scope," "project plan," "timeline", "PMO tools" or "status report."

Hint: An increasing number of companies are using "agile" methodologies for developing new products or services. Agile aims to increase the amount of time doing instead of planning. The points listed above are still generally valid, except that iterative "sprints" reduce the importance of upfront planning and that planning and progress tracking takes place in so called "agile ceremonies."

Hint: Signoffs sound bureaucratic, but they do help to ensure that everyone is on the same page. Every minute invested in communication and signoffs at the start of a project saves you five later on.

Hint: Projects usually have "steering committees," "project review boards" or similar meetings with very senior stakeholders. Invest time in bilateral meetings with your most important stakeholders <u>beforehand</u> to answer all their questions and ensure they are on board. Even though this may seem like a waste of time, an unexpected question or critical feedback in a steering committee can result in weeks of extra work or budget cuts for your project. It's better to align everyone beforehand.

The big meeting with very senior stakeholders should ideally be a mere formality since you already aligned the most important attendees beforehand.

※ ※ ※

58. Reuse as much as possible.

If you're asked to create a business case, sales offer, contract draft, market analysis or audit report – don't start from scratch. Either recycle your previous work or ask colleagues for input (past examples, company templates, formats, guidelines etc.). Talking to your colleagues is especially helpful as they are likely to have worked on something similar. Ten minutes of picking their brain can be more effective than a day of thinking about how to structure a problem. Your worst-case scenario is Googling for reusable content and adjusting it to your specific task. Just don't plagiarize as you can get yourself and your company in a lot of trouble.

Reusing content doesn't only save you time, it also increases the likelihood of your work being accepted. Your boss will have certain expectations as to what a business case/market analysis etc. should look like. The closer you are to their expectations or industry standards, the more comfortable your boss will feel with your work.

※ ※ ※

59. Pause and use the power of silence.

If a pause in conversation lasts for more than 4 seconds, pop-psychology says that we begin to feel uncomfortable and will say something break the awkward silence. Use that to your advantage. Instead of asking questions, just pause whenever you want the other party to say something. It works like magic.

Hint: If the silence becomes awkward, you can always ask prompting questions such as "How do you think we can solve this?" or "What do you think?"

***

60. Ask "is there anything else ... ?"

This question can save you hundreds of hours over the span of your career. If you ever have to take over a new task, interview someone, or holding a meeting, ask "is there anything else I should know?" or "is there anything else you would like to tell me?"
Then sit back and wait.
You'll be surprised at how much valuable information you will get from this one simple question. Given time to think and asked to offer up anything else on their mind, people will usually remember some information which they would otherwise not have provided you with.

***

61. Face time > phone > email.

If you want to resolve an issue quickly and effectively, have a face-to-face meeting. People can't ignore a personal visit and are also generally more open to sharing information or less likely to make up excuses when talking to you in person. Their body language can also reveal much more than a call or email ever could.
If you can't get a face-to-face meeting, use your phone. Calls allow you to discuss a wide range of topics more quickly and in greater depth than an email ever could. Calls also take a lot less time to prepare for than formulating long, structured emails. Irrespective of whether it's an in-person meeting, a phone call,

or an email, always establish a personal relationship with the other party by making small talk.

Hint: Only use email if you want to have written documentation of your interaction (i.e. if you want to CYA – "Cover Your Ass").

62. Ask "is now a good time?"

If you're calling a colleague or dropping by their office unannounced and need >2 minutes of their time, ask them "is now a good time?" This simple question makes you sound highly considerate and enables your "ambushed" colleague to politely postpone your request if they are very busy.

63. Make your calls in the first half of the day.

Colleagues are typically in a better mood and more likely to say yes to requests in the first half of the day. Make use of that and call them in the morning.
Remember the saying, "You attract more flies with honey than with vinegar"? Being pleasant and courteous when calling makes a real difference.
Hint: This also goes for calls to other companies and your private calls to doctors' offices or public institutions. Employees and receptionists are much friendlier and helpful at the start of their day than in the afternoon.

64. State what you're calling about at the beginning.

Don't be the type of caller that directly launches into a five-minute monologue without letting the other person get a word in edgewise. What sometimes happens is that you're speaking to the wrong person, but they haven't been able to tell you during your five-minute monologue.

Instead, simply start your call with "I wanted to talk about [insert topic here]. Are you the right person to talk to?" If you're not speaking to the right person, the other party can quickly refer you to someone better-suited, saving you both time and unnecessary frustration.

65. Leave good voicemails.

Nothing is worse than getting a voicemail where you don't know who called, why they called and how to contact them. When leaving a voicemail, say your name, who you are, what you're calling about, how urgent it is, and how to reach you. It's that simple.

66. Use Google images more.

Office work typically involves creating a lot of presentations or written documents. This hack helps you if you're suffering from writer's block or can't think of a good way to visualize a topic. Clicking individual links from a Google search is not very efficient – especially if you need to scan through lengthy texts or pdfs. By looking at the image search results instead, you can quickly find a wide range of charts, tables and visualizations.

Browsing image search results is also a good idea as a lot of thought is put into how to succinctly visually introduce or portray topics – allowing you to quickly understand the most important terms, categories, and figures for whatever topic you're researching. You will also get inspired by how other companies visually portray their team, the benefits of their product or next steps. Once you find relevant images, you can always dive into the websites, articles or studies behind them.

Hint: By looking at the image search results, you will also see what pictures are most commonly associated with your topic. This is especially important if you are trying to communicate with or sell to the general public.

✶ ✶ ✶

67. Chew gum when you need to concentrate.

Chewing gum increases the blood flow to your brain and has been scientifically proven to help you concentrate longer.

Hint: Chew a gum with a strong flavor (e.g. cinnamon) while learning and when you need to recall the newly learnt information. By chewing a gum of the same flavor at both times, you are using the same memory centers that bring back powerful nostalgic memories based on no more than a faint smell or taste.

✶ ✶ ✶

68. Use earplugs or headphones to concentrate.

The trend towards open offices has resulted in a huge increase in the ambient noise level. You now have to concentrate while listening to other people crushing ice cubes between their teeth, cutting nails or humming songs. Even if you have a small office, sirens, barking dogs and construction work can be distracting. Having earplugs or noise cancelling headphones can really help sometimes. You'll feel much calmer and focused wearing them. Keep in mind that with earplugs you'll still be able to hear conversations and talk on the phone. With noise cancelling headphones however, you will hear nothing except your music.

Hint: If you buy earplugs, go for some that are attached to a lanyard. You can easily remove or insert them and won't have to

search for individual earplugs.
Hint: Ask a colleague to check whether your headphones "leak" sound while you're listening to music. Otherwise, any person nearby can also hear exactly what you're listening to.

69. Learn to ignore emails.

Sometimes the best reply is none at all. It may sound bad, but sometimes it is beneficial to just ignore some emails (especially if you are just on CC). The person who sent the email usually finds an alternative solution without your input and matters settle themselves. Naturally, you should reply if you get a follow-up or escalation email.
Hint: Don't start ignoring <u>all</u> your emails. That can only result in you ignoring a really important email. The trick is to quickly skim each email and see if you can selectively ignore it.

70. Only hold meetings with clear goals.

Take a few minutes to really think about what outcomes you need from a meeting, why you need them (i.e. what for) and who you need to invite. Only then should you formulate your meeting goals – the more specific you are, the smoother your meeting will be. Be sure to list your meeting goals very explicitly in your invitation email so that participants are better able to prepare or can suggest other people who should also be invited. You should also be explicit in telling your attendees what you expect of them and what they need to prepare for your meeting. Nothing is more frustrating than having meetings and finding out that you need to wait another week because some attendees didn't prepare.

Set a good example by making sure that you're prepared – hold yourself to the same standards that you hold others to.
Hint: You can save a lot of your own time by only attending meetings which also have clear goals or agendas. If you are invited to a vague meeting, be sure to ask for more information. In some cases you may not even be required or can send someone else, freeing up valuable time in your calendar.

***

71. Make meetings have an irregular length.

Meetings are typically 30, 60 or 120 minutes long. Create meetings with an irregular length of 20, 45 or 75 minutes. Any multiple of 5 is fine. Generally, you should also aim for shorter rather than longer durations. Not only will your meeting invites stand out, participants will also be more focused as they are more aware of the limited time than usual.
This hack also makes use of the "psychological pricing" principle, which is behind all those irregular $0.99, $3.33 or $8.88 prices. We know that 99 cents is just about the same as a dollar, just as we know that 45 minutes are nearly the same as 60 minutes. Meetings with irregular durations are psychologically rounded down and perceived as being significantly less of a time investment, meaning your meeting invites are more likely to be accepted.

***

72. Make meetings as big as necessary but as small as possible.

Instead of having five meetings with different people and then having to ensure everyone is on the same page, just have one big meeting with everyone. People may complain, but in the end, it really is better for you (and your company). Look at successful executives; they always seem to be having large meetings. This is because they know the advantages of having everyone together in a room are much greater than the individual complaints of those who don't want to attend.

Hint: Do not hold <u>unnecessarily</u> large meetings. If you gain a reputation as someone who holds unnecessary meetings, people will quickly start declining your invitations. Think about what you want to achieve and who you need to do that – then send out invitations. Explicitly state who you invited (and <u>why</u>) in the invitation email or at the beginning of the meeting.

73. Isolate topics if they are not relevant to meetings.

If you ever want to sabotage a meeting, there is no better way than to bring in new topics which are related to the overall issue at hand but not to the goals of that particular meeting. The best countermeasure is to isolate such topics and proceed with the meeting's original goals.

For example, say a meeting participant is derailing your meeting by talking about all the intricacies of an IT-system (despite this being not relevant for 80% of participants). Deescalate the situation by using phrases such as "I don't want to lose the good point you're making, but let's save it for the moment to focus on…" or "Let's discuss it bilaterally after this meeting as this discussion is not relevant to everyone here today."

74. End meetings if you achieved what you wanted.

If your meeting was supposed to take an hour and you've reached all your meeting goals in the first fifteen minutes, thank everyone for attending and end the meeting. It makes you look efficient and will earn you the respect of others who are grateful for newly freed-up time.

This is not to say that you should end meetings immediately and not engage in a bit of small talk towards the end of meetings. Use your judgement – if you are small tight-knit group and haven't caught up recently, proceed differently than if you have twenty busy people in front of you.

75. Keep (and share) to-do lists for project and meetings.

A continuously updated to-do list containing all open issues or tasks ensures that no one can claim they didn't know what they had to do. Be sure to write down an owner and deadline for every single to-do and share your list often.

Sending around to-do lists after meetings and keeping track of the to-dos in subsequent meetings will garner you a reputation for staying on top of things and saves everyone a lot time.

76. Sort your notes into (I) - (A) - (D).

Reviewing your meeting notes is a lot easier if you label each point as (I)nformation, (A)ction or (D)ecision. Any point labelled as an (A)ction point is a ToDo you need to take care of. This hack is best explained using an example for a meeting on the new marketing campaign:

- (I) Marketing budget of 1 million US$ allocated for next year
- (D) 500k US$ to be spent on digital marketing, 500k US$ on print and TV (decided by Michelle)

- (A) Contact XYZ marketing firm for price quote on Instagram campaign
- (A) Create overview of TV stations and prices
- (A) Present final marketing strategy to management on 28th of June

77. Use pictures to save time.

Don't waste your time documenting when you can have an instant protocol with a single picture. If you've done a hands-on workshop with lots of post-its flying around or your boss has sketched out what you need to do next, simply take a picture with your smartphone. Such pictures can be easily attached to meeting protocols/minutes or directly pasted into PowerPoint presentations.
Hint: You can also use your smartphone if you don't want to collect business cards at conventions. Just take a picture of the business card owner holding up his card. It makes transferring contact details to Outlook and remembering the person much easier. Be aware that in some cultures, this may not be polite.

78. Get replies to cold call emails.

In order to increase your chances of getting an answer from someone you don't know personally, search for their name on Google to see how your email can stand out. Reference an article or study by the person you're contacting or ask them a thoughtful question about it. To increase your chances of a reply, you can also offer to introduce them to someone you know or ask if they will be at an industry convention or other event you will also be attending. People usually reply if they know they will meet you in person at a future date.

Be sure to include very explicitly what you want from the person you're writing.

Example:

Dear Dr. Rockwell,

I am a software developer at Widget Company and am currently working on an autonomous driving solution. We are looking to hire a deep learning specialist. Do you know someone or could you recommend how best to find good candidates?

The reason I am reaching out to you is that your articles on the future of autonomous driving have really resonated with me and my colleagues. We were very excited over your recent breakthrough in the automatic prediction of pedestrian behavior. |or| Do you know Dr. Smith? She leads car autonomy initiatives at Car Company Inc. and would probably have some interesting market insights for you. I could introduce you if you'd like. |or| Will you be at the Las Vegas "Automotive Autonomy Convention" on the 12th of September? I would be very glad to meet you in person.

Hint: You never know why someone didn't reply to your email, but sometimes people (especially the very busy ones) just miss, accidentally delete or forget your email. If you don't get an answer to your email within a week, it doesn't hurt to send a follow-up email to prompt a response.

Hint: There is always a fine line between being persistent and being annoying if you don't get replies. Generally, you should keep trying as you are likely to get a reply at some point – if only to stop you from contacting them. When sending a new email, have your previously unanswered emails attached below. If calling, you can say that you already wrote an email and go from there.

79. Organize your workspace.

A key component of doing work as efficiently as possible is to keep your paper and digital documents organized. Having a system will massively reduce the time you spend searching for things. Searching is never fun, especially when someone else urgently needs whatever you're desperately trying to find.

There is no one-size-fits-all approach. A typical approach is to name folders after departments or projects or people or dates and sort documents accordingly. You should use whatever structure is closest to the way you organize your work in your head.

For organizing individual files, a good idea is having the date as the first part of your filename ("YYYYMMDD_") and the document version as the last part ("_draft" or "_sent"). For example, a contract sent on the 1st of May 2017 would be named "20170501_Contract_sent".

Starting filenames with dates allows you to quickly sort or search documents (searching for "20170501*" in Windows will show all documents related to the 1st of May 2017). For consistency purposes, you should not use the current date but a constant date related to the document (i.e. even if you wrote a first draft of the contract on the 20th of April, the filename should be "20170501_Contract_draft").

Ending your filenames with a document version will help you efficiently differentiate between internal drafts and final document versions. You can typically count up from "_v1," "_v2," "_v3" or "_v1.1," "_v1.2," "_v1.3" as well as differentiate "_draft," "_sent," and "_protocol" versions. It is generally a good idea to create new versions often to avoid losing work or to trace back changes you previously made.

Hint: Ask what the organizing and naming standards are for your office. If there are none, then ensure that your team adopts the same standards. Otherwise, collaboration will not be as fun as it could be.

80. Drink coffee slowly.

According to studies, you should drink your coffee slowly over the course of a few hours to remain on a caffeine plateau and avoid a "caffeine crash." This works best if you have a thermos cup which keeps your coffee hot for a few hours. Otherwise, green tea is recommended to give you an equal energy boost, but with a lesser crash later on.
Most energy drinks are not a good idea. Despite being stimulating, they are full of sugar. Sugar causes your insulin to spike and greatly increases the crash later on.

81. Avoid the post-lunch drowsiness.

Experiment with a few simple changes to avoid becoming tired or unfocused after lunch. With these changes, you should be full of energy for those afternoon meetings:

- Avoid foods high in sugar or flour-based foods (pasta, bread, muffins etc.). These cause your insulin to spike

- Avoid foods high in fat as these take longer and are more difficult to digest

- Steer towards vegetables, whole wheat pasta, rice, quinoa, chickpeas, eggs, as well as chicken, turkey, or tuna. These are good sources of energy

- Take a 5-10 minute walk after eating to increase the blood circulation to your digestive system
- Eat smaller portions as the energy drain caused by digesting is correspondingly lower
- Eat a healthy breakfast. A majority of those who suffer from post-lunch drowsiness eat no or only an unhealthy breakfast (e.g. high-sugar cereals)
- Use coffee or chewing gum as a quick fix if you couldn't avoid an unhealthy lunch

IT OFFICE HACKS

Emails and office software are necessary evils for working in offices. The hacks listed below can help you avoid wrongly sent emails, speed up your work at the computer and make you look like a real IT-expert to the rest of the office. Generally speaking, these hacks are also applicable to non-Microsoft products – use Google to find out how to apply them to your specific operating system or software!

82. Search for solved IT problems.

When trying to solve an IT problem by doing a Google search, include the words "solved" or "solution" in your search. That way, you get search results where someone was able to resolve the very problem you also have.

★★★

83. Delay sent emails by 1 Minute.

Set up a rule in Outlook that delays the sending of emails by 1 minute. Even if you clicked "send," your email remains in your outbox for a precious 60 seconds, during which you can still delete it. To learn how to set up such a rule, just Google "delay email sending outlook rule." You may not need such a delay for 99% of emails, but for that 1% of mistakenly or prematurely sent emails, it will be worth it.

★★★

84. Recall emails.

You can delete emails you mistakenly sent or in cases where you accidentally clicked "reply to all" instead of just "reply." If the recipient also uses Outlook and hasn't opened your email yet, your email will be deleted from their inbox. Outlook will tell you if the recall was successful or not for each recipient.

To learn how to recall an email in Outlook, just Google "recall email outlook."

Hint: Recalling emails doesn't always work. If you can't recall an email, just send a second email asking the recipient to delete the previous email which you mistakenly sent. Sending such a follow-up email is always a good idea. Either the recipient complies with your deletion request or you just helped cover your ass (such an email shows that you did everything in your power to mitigate the negative effects of your mistakenly sent email).

Hint: Contact your boss if the email you mistakenly sent contains highly sensitive data (e.g., home addresses of colleagues or internal notes on which customers are being charged too much). The quicker you can go into damage control mode, the better.

85. Use follow-ups for emails.

Outlook has a "follow-up" function which can be added to emails you send. Adding such a "follow-up" makes a reminder automatically appear in the Outlook calendar. To learn how to do this, you can Google "add follow up reminder in Outlook." There are two forms these follow-ups can take:

- Firstly, you can add follow-ups to recipients of emails, so that when your email says, "please get back to me by 15:00 on the 20th of March," your recipients will have a reminder pop-up in their calendars at exactly 15:00 on the 20th of March.

- Secondly, you can add follow-ups to outgoing emails which result in reminders popping up in <u>your calendar</u>, but not in the calendars of recipients. It's useful when you send an email containing a question or request and want to remind yourself to follow up 10 days later.

86. Never forget your emails & internet usage are monitored.

When using your company email account or browsing the web on a work computer, keep in mind that everything may be recorded and archived somewhere. Even on the off chance that emails aren't monitored, it's a good rule of thumb to act like they are (especially since WikiLeaks showed that the NSA intercepts all of your personal and professional emails, text messages and phone calls).

Better to have a coffee and talk in person than have to endure an HR employee reading out your very explicit account of what happened in Las Vegas.

Hint: Just like some companies use software to monitor your internet usage, some companies use software to search all company emails for inappropriate content. Sending around dirty jokes with swearwords may just flag your email account for HR. These days, anything can be considered offensive, so you don't want your company emails (which are usually legal property of the company!) to implicate you.

87. Learn keyboard shortcuts.

It is surprising how many employees don't know the most common shortcuts on Windows computers. Shortcuts will really save you a lot of time, and the sooner you learn them, the better. Listed below are some of the most common ones; you can always Google "complete list of keyboard shortcuts" if you are interested in learning more. If you don't know where a button is located, Google it and then look at the image results. **Hint:** Naturally, you don't have to learn all these overnight. Even picking up on some of the shortcuts will increase your efficiency at work and make you look like a computer wizard to your colleagues.

Microsoft Windows shortcuts

- **Alt + Tab**: Quickly switch between programs. Especially useful if you're writing a personal email or shopping while at work
- **Alt + Esc**: Cycle between open windows (i.e. minimized programs are not included)
- **⊞ + D** or **⊞ + M**: Automatically minimize all windows and show the desktop.
- **PrtScr**: Take a screenshot of your computer screen. In order to save the screenshot, you may have to copy it into an image editing program like Microsoft Paint first
- **⊞**: Open the Windows start menu
- **⊞ + L**: Lock your computer

Most Office programs (Outlook, Excel, PowerPoint, Word etc.)

- **Ctrl + A**: Select all
- **Ctrl + X**: Cut
- **Ctrl + C**: Copy
- **Ctrl + V**: Paste
- **Ctrl + F**: Find
- **Ctrl + S**: Save
- **Ctrl + O**: Open
- **Ctrl + Z**: Undo last change
- **Ctrl + Y**: Redo last change
- **Ctrl + N**: Open a new window
- **Alt + F4** or **Ctrl + Q**: Quit
- **PageUp**: Scroll up
- **PageDown**: Scroll down
- **Ctrl + Home**: Scroll to the start
- **Ctrl + End**: Scroll to the end
- **Ctrl + F2**: Print preview
- **F1**: Help
- **F2**: Rename a file or folder
- **F3**: Search
- **F7**: Spellcheck
- **F11**: Show as full screen
- **F12**: Save as
- **Ctrl + P**: Print
- **Ctrl + Mouse wheel**: Zoom in and out

Text-formatting shortcuts

- **Ctrl + B**: Make text bold

- **Ctrl + I**: Italicize text
- **Ctrl + U**: Underline text
- **Shift + F3**: Change between uppercasing / capitalizing or lowercasing highlighted text
- **Shift + Enter**: Go to a new line without creating a new paragraph (called a line break)

Outlook shortcuts

- **Ctrl + 1**: Switch to mail
- **Ctrl + 2**: Switch to calendar
- **Ctrl + 3**: Switch to contacts
- **Ctrl + Shift + A**: Create an appointment
- **Ctrl + Shift + Q**: Create a meeting request
- **Ctrl + Shift + C**: Create a contact
- **Ctrl + Shift + M**: Create a new email
- **Ctrl + E** or **F3**: Search
- **F9**: Refresh inbox / outbox
- **Ctrl + U**: Mark as unread
- **Ctrl + R**: Reply to an email
- **Ctrl + Shift + R**: Reply to all
- **Alt + S**: Send

PowerPoint shortcuts

- **F5**: Enter presentation mode (start of presentation)
- **Shift + F5**: Enter presentation mode (current slide)
- **B**: Switch to a black screen when in presentation mode
- **Ctrl + D**: Duplicate the currently selected item
- **Ctrl + move item with mouse**: Duplicates the selected item

- **Ctrl + Shift + move item with mouse**: Duplicates the selected item along a straight horizontal or vertical path
- **Arrow keys** (up, down, left, right): Move the selected item

Excel shortcuts

- **Ctrl + Arrow keys** (up, down, left, right): Move to the last cell in your column / row
- **Ctrl + Shift + Arrow keys** (up, down, left, right): Select all cells in your column / row
- **Ctrl + End**: Move to the cell at the bottom right of your table
- **Ctrl + Page Down / Page Up**: Move to the next / previous worksheet
- **Ctrl + 1**: Open the format cell window
- **Ctrl + K**: Open the insert Hyperlink window
- **Shift + F2**: Create a note
- **Ctrl + E**: Excel flashfills cells with the pattern it automatically recognized
- **F4**: Fixate the cell referenced when writing a formula
- **F7**: Spellcheck the sheet or selected cells

Internet browser shortcuts

- **F5 / Ctrl + R**: Refreshes the page you're on
- **F6 / Alt + D**: Selects the address bar
- **Ctrl + T**: Opens a new tab
- **Ctrl + W**: Closes the current tab you're on
- **Ctrl + D**: Bookmark the site you're browsing
- **Ctrl + Shift + T**: Re-opens the last tab you closed
- **Backspace**: Navigates back to the last page you visited
- **Ctrl + Tab**: Cycle between the different tabs

Adobe PDF Reader specific

- **F11**: Enable / disable fullscreen mode
- **Ctrl + 6**: Add a stick note / comment
- **Ctrl + 8**: Show all comments

✶✶✶

88. Use the Quick Access Toolbar (QAT).

Microsoft Office programs like Word, PowerPoint and Excel enable you to create your own QAT. This QAT is always visible and enables you to quickly access (hence the name) your 20+ most commonly used functions. Google "quick access toolbar + [software]" to find out how to do this for your office software. You can also Google "quick access toolbar + [your job]" to see how others have personalized their QATs. This can be especially useful if you work as a controller, editor or publisher.

✶✶✶

89. Search multiple PDFs at once.

Open Adobe PDF reader and use "Shift + Ctrl + F" to search multiple PDFs. Otherwise put all the PDFs you want to search in a folder and use the windows explorer search (top right hand corner) to find all the PDFs which contain the search term you are looking for. This will make your life a lot easier than opening and searching through each PDF individually (something often seen in the office).
Hint: This only works for non-encrypted PDFs and PDFs with searchable text. Handwritten notes or text within graphics are not included in the PDF search, unless made readable using OCR (optical character recognition).

✶✶✶

90. AutoRecover is your best friend.

Office can help you avoid having to redo work which was lost due to a computer crash or power outage. Simply configure Office to automatically save your work every few minutes. You can set the number of minutes yourself, saving at least once every ten minutes is recommended. The more often you save, the slower the program is.

In order to setup autosaving, go to "File → Options → Save" and then check the box which says "Save AutoRecover information every [x] minutes".

If an office program didn't close correctly, AutoRecover versions are sometimes shown. Just open the most recently saved version and you're set. Should you accidentally close the window showing AutoRecover versions or forget to save the autorecovered version, you can find them under "File →Information → Manage Document → Recover unsaved documents".

91. Use auto-correct to quickly write emails or documents.

You can save a lot of time and typing by abbreviating phrases or names you commonly use and letting auto-correct write out the full phrase or name. "Best regards" can be abbreviated as "BR", "sincerely yours" as "SY", "thank you for your reply" can become "TYR" etc. You can also abbreviate your name, department name or colleagues name to avoid having to type them out each time. Open Outlook and go to "File → Options → Email → Spelling and Autocorrect". You should then see a table with two columns, one titled "replace" and the other "with." Enter a memorable but unique abbreviation in the "replace" column and whatever phrase or name you type frequently in the "with" column.

Depending on your operating system, you may also have to manually adjust autocorrect in Word, PowerPoint, or Excel – and not just Outlook.

Hint: Auto-correct also works on your iOS or Android smartphone. If you are prone to misspelling on your phone's tiny keyboard, this hack is really useful.

★★★

92. Create one-click conference calls.

The 1800 123123 phone number with pin code 667788# can be replaced with 1800123123,,667788#. Separate the phone number and pin code with two commas and anyone with a smartphone can dial in with one simple click.

★★★

93. Learn macros.

A lot of office work involves using Excel or Word. By learning how to write macros, you can automate repetitive tasks. Just be sure to save a backup copy in case you make a mistake when programming your macro.

Hint: If you Google "learn office macros" you will find a lot of resources on the basics. If you have a specific task you want to automate, then Google is also your best friend. Just search for "macro + [whatever you're trying to do]" and in 99% of cases, you'll find a solution. To save time in the long run, you can create your own collection of macros that you use often.

★★★

94. Tag your Outlook contacts.

Add personal notes to your Outlook contacts to jog your memory. Such notes can be on the contact's expertise, responsibilities, or even personal details (e.g., had a son in 2018). An added benefit of your personal notes is that they can also be searched for in Outlook, enabling you to quickly find your "expert on ball bearings" or "marketing headhunter."

95. Turn your email signature into a small advertisement.

You'll probably be sending out thousands of emails each year. Instead of just having your contact details in your email signature, consider adding links or pictures to it. These links or picture should interest your customers ("Interested in insurance analytics? Click here" or "Click here to read about our newest thinking on robotics"). Regularly update your signature if you are launching a new product or marketing campaign, or have an upcoming event you want to highlight.
Hint: To find out how to change your email signature in Outlook, just Google it ("change email signature outlook"). If you work in a large company, there may be strict rules regarding email signatures – so check first.

96. Backup files in the cloud or a second hard drive.

Check your company's IT policy regarding backups to avoid losing your work due to a broken computer or flooded office.
For files, you can use cloud-based solutions such as Google Drive, Microsoft OneDrive or Dropbox (Edward Snowden recommends staying away from Dropbox). You can also store files on a (password-protected) USB hard drive. Just be sure to get an OK from your IT colleagues first.
Hint: You can also backup files or notes by adding them to an email addressed to yourself. You can also write but never send

such backup emails to save them in your "drafts" folder. Be aware that in some email programs you need to press "save" or "Ctrl + S" to save drafts.

97. Try out cloud-based note or project management software.

Cloud-based note managers like keep.google.com or Evernote.com enable you to quickly search and categorize your notes as well as share them with others. Cloud-based project management or software development solutions enable a much greater collaboration between team members. There are hundreds of solutions available, so you can check to see which is best for your specific industry and company. Some of the more common ones are Slack, Trello, Zoho, Confluence or Jira.

GETTING A GOOD ROUTINE

After your first few days at the office, you want to get a good routine going. A good routine is all about looking highly promotable while simultaneously doing the least amount of drudge work necessary. Look for colleagues that have been at your office for a long time – the smart ones will have developed their own routines which you can imitate!

98. Ask for what you want.

This is one of the most important general pointers for putting your career onto the fast track. The future belongs to the askers. The future does not belong to those who wish and hope that their lives will (magically) improve. Step up and ask for what you want. If you don't get it, ask again and again until you do.

∗ ∗ ∗

99. Steer your work towards activities you enjoy.

This may sound like a no-brainer, but very often, people don't proactively seek out opportunities to do activities they enjoy at work. Take a few minutes and write down what activities you would enjoy doing at work – be it drawing, writing, organizing, travelling or holding presentations.
For example, if you enjoy writing, try finding as many opportunities to write at work as possible – volunteer for writing tasks and tell colleagues to contact you each time a task involving writing comes up.

By steering your work towards things you enjoy, work becomes more fun. Having fun makes it easier to hone your skills and become a valuable expert.

100. Stay positive.

No matter what happens, keep a positive attitude. No one wants to work with a cynical pessimist or be miserable for 8 hours a day. Even if the work itself is nothing to be optimistic about, you should at least maintain a good mood. Your colleagues, customers and bosses will be grateful that you're making the office a more enjoyable place to work.

101. Re-frame how you see work.

If you think your job is boring, you will fall victim to this self-fulfilling prophecy. You will be unhappy and unsuccessful at work. Re-framing how you see work is all about motivating yourself and finding the small, hidden joys in your daily routines. Re-frame your work into a game or challenge to appeal to your natural enjoyment of "play" activities. Try to "gamify" your work as much as possible – every task, every deadline, every email, etc.

Think of your work activities as a series of small games – how fast can you answer calls, how many documents can you review in an hour, how many customers can you help per day etc. You can even think of imaginary scores and points with which to reward yourself.

You can also try to think of your work as a series of small challenges or competitions such as: can I create an excel worksheet with no errors, can I get more sales than I did yesterday, etc.

The more of your work you re-frame as a game or challenge, the more motivated and focused you will be.

Hint: It's better if you set yourself small challenges and beat them. Don't set yourself a challenge of creating a complex business case in Excel from scratch – aim for completing 15 cells, then the next 15 (and so on). The more you break down a task into smaller pieces, the easier, more manageable and rewarding your challenges become.

Hint: By rewarding yourself after completing challenges, you can develop a "Pavlovian reflex"; you can train your brain to become addicted to and even enjoy challenges. Reward yourself with candy, surf the internet for a few minutes, have a chat with a colleague or just get up and take a small stroll.

102. Build yourself a "talent stack."

Employees with a "talent stack" are much more valuable and well paid. You can hack your way to success by learning a combination of useful talents (i.e. a "talent stack") that will differentiate you from your peers. In most offices, combining an above-average knowledge of marketing, presenting, sales, controlling and IT will turbocharge your career. You don't need to become an expert in any of these areas – just have an above-average understanding. Build you own talent stack early on by learning as much as possible and look outside your own department.

Hint: Learning a talent stack doesn't mean having to retake university classes or read mountains of books. Ask people from other departments to teach you about their field of expertise or volunteer for projects which include new topics you would like to learn about.

103. Learn to present.

Presenting an idea well greatly increase its chances of success. A very important presentation can make a bigger difference to your career and salary than that initial interview you spent weeks preparing for. Listed below are the most common tips for presenting well.

- **Posture:** Feet hip-width apart, stand up straight.
- **Hands:** Keep your hands at your sides. If this feels very unnatural, hold a laser pointer or a clicker to switch between slides.
- **Gesture:** Use big, open gestures. Avoid hasty pointing or gesturing too fast.
- **Movement**: The most common advice of standing still can seem a little unnatural. If you feel the need to move, look to where you want to move, then move 1-2 seconds later. This puts your audience at ease since you have signaled your intent to move <u>before</u> moving. Avoid rocking from side to side, this make you seem nervous and inexperienced.
- **Facial expression**: Keep a smile on your face. A smile radiates confidence and puts your audience at ease. Look interested in what you are presenting and show passion.
- **Voice**: Vary your voice in tone and volume to make your presentation more interesting and highlight key points

vocally. Avoid presenting in a monotonous, uninteresting voice. Don't speak too quickly.

- **Eye contact**: Look at people when the presentation content is especially relevant to them or when mentioning them. Don't switch who you are looking at mid-sentence. Avoid scanning the audience, instead look at individual people for 2-3 seconds then move on – this makes your audience feel more engaged and your presentation more personal.

- **Less text is more**: Your presentation won't be effective if your audience has to listen to you and simultaneously read a wall of text. Try to keep your presentation as visual as possible. Ideally cover only one topic or aspect per PowerPoint slide. Only in rare circumstances can you go up to 3 topics – anything more than 3 topics is too complex for your audience. Search YouTube for Ted Talks or presentations given by Elon Musk or Steve Jobs for inspiration.

- **Choice of words**: Keep sentences short and simple. Add adjectives to make your topic more interesting. Use your limited time to focus on the key issues. Even though you may want to explain all the details, you will usually overwhelm your audience.

- **Pauses**: Build in 1-3 second pauses at the end of sentences. Add longer pauses at key points. This may seem unnatural, but it gives your presentation more weight and gravitas. Your audience also has more time to reflect on and process what you said.

- **Call-to-actions**: At the end of your speech, directly state what you want your audience to do.
  Do you want them to contact you? Then end your speech on the last slide titled "Let's talk!" with your contact details in huge font below.
  Do you want them to remember the new company values? End your speech by repeating the memorable values shown on your last slide.

- **Questions**: There are two schools of thought on this. One says to ask your audience to hold onto questions until the end so that you can stay on message during your speech. The other school says to accept questions during your speech to heighten audience interaction and steer your speech towards the topics your audience is interested in. Try both and see what works best for you.

For guidance, here are the five most common presenting mistakes:

- Speaking too quickly and not using pauses to give your listeners the chance to absorb or reflect on what you said.

- Not showing any emotion – if you don't show any passion or externally discernable interest in your own presentation, why should your audience care?

- Unnecessary "ahs," "uhs" and "uhms". Practice until you no longer use them.

- Complex, run-on sentences with lots of connector words (and, so, but, then etc.)

- Repeating yourself ("as I said before", "as seen earlier" etc.). Use repetition only to highlight key points you are trying to make.

Hint: For very important presentations, you should practice. Film yourself or ask an experienced friend or colleague. Then use YouTube or Google to find advice on specific aspects (e.g., "how to have a more powerful voice" or "how to have a less monotonous voice").

Hint: If someone in your company presents well, pay attention to their mannerisms and adopt some of them. Otherwise, find a politician or other public figure and study a few speeches of theirs.

Hint: According to Dr. Albert Mehrabian's studies, the power and credibility of your speech depends on three factors: 55% of your credibility depends on your body language/visual impression as a presenter, 38% on your voice and tone and <u>only</u> 7% on your choice of words. In phone calls, 85% of your credibility is determined by your voice and tone. Only 15% of your caller's impression of your speech depends on your choice of words.

104. Master digital presentations.

COVID-19 has only accelerated the shift to digital meetings. Listed below is advice to improve your digital presentation skills:

- Put the webcam at eye level – you don't want someone looking at the bottom of your chin or up your nose. If using a laptop, put a few books underneath

- Put the webcam at arm's length from your face. This is the natural distance for business conversations in most countries

- Combine bounced lighting (a ceiling lamp or floor lamp nearby) with direct lighting (a light behind your webcam pointed at your face). Make sure the light pointed at your face doesn't blind you or you will spend your presentation squinting at your virtual audience

- Look at the webcam when talking. This creates the impression that you are looking directly at your audience
- Take pauses when looking at notes. This allows for your audience to reflect on what you said
- Smile
- Use fewer gestures than you would in an offline presentation
- Make sure the technology works beforehand. No one enjoys having to wait.

105. Be visual.

Why do companies spend billions of dollars on advertising via pictures and videos? Because it works! The same goes for your own work. If you want to persuade your employees, peers and bosses, you should try to be visual. Use inspiring pictures which show what the world will be after your idea or vision is implemented. Create a few visually compelling screens of the app you are trying to pitch instead of writing a long conceptual paper. Add a short video of customer testimonials when requesting a budget to expand your product line. You get the picture ☺.

106. Learn "smart" questions which you can ask anytime.

Listed below are several questions which <u>can</u> make you sound smart and be asked in most situations – adapt them to your specific situation. You can also use these questions to fluster a potential office rival's presentation, but be aware that they may do the same to you.

- Why did you choose [topic]? Why did you personally start [topic]? How does this fit in with our strategy/ mission/ values?

- What approaches/ strategies are you using and why? What is the one thing you would change? If anything was possible, what would you do?

- How could [topic] fail? What are your main challenges? What obstacles do you expect?

- What is your main objective? How do you measure success? How will you know you've been successful?

- What's next for [topic]? How do you expect to evolve [topic] further? What is the long-term vision? How can we scale [topic] further?

- On a scale of 1 to 10, how important is...? How would you compare [topic] to [competitor]? How does your [topic] differentiate itself from other solutions?

- What question have you been asked the most so far? What matters most to you? What were your biggest "lessons learned"?

Hint: Asking questions is not always a good idea. Nobody wants to sit there while someone else asks inane questions just to seem smart or interested. So, avoid asking questions unless you think the answer may be of use to the majority of people attending. Also, avoid asking questions towards the end of a meeting, especially if the meeting is on a Friday afternoon or already overrun its scheduled end. Ask your questions bilaterally instead – via email or phone.

107. Give more compliments.

Mark Twain famously said, "I can live for two months on a good compliment." While not factually true, it does show how much of a difference a compliment can make.

Study after study has shown that giving compliments is beneficial for everyone involved. Receiving a compliment reduces your stress levels, improves your cognitive performance, increases your motivation, increases your self-esteem and increases your overall happiness with life (including out of the office). Giving a compliment boosts your happiness and increases the quality of your relationship with the person you complimented.

Giving lots of compliments also helps change the environment of your workplace – wouldn't you rather work in an office where compliments are the norm instead of the exception?

Enough about the theory. Let's dive into how to give a good compliment:

- **Be authentic.** Humans are good at identifying fake compliments. Instead of counterproductive false flattery, try to find something that you really find praiseworthy about the person you want to compliment.

- **Personality not performance.** People who receive compliments on their personality are happier than when complimented on their performance. Use "you're such a creative person – good job!" instead of "you did such a creative job!".

- **Be specific**. A compliment about a specific event or task makes the compliment more genuine. The person receiving the compliment can also better act on your compliment and is not left confused about what they did to merit your praise.
- **Don't wait**. Compliment someone shortly after they have done something great – don't wait too long.
- **Take your time**. "Drive-by" compliments are better than nothing, but you should take your time to show your appreciation. Plan 5 minutes to have a real conversation and connection with the person you are complimenting.
- **Do it often**. After having been in school and university system where the majority of focus has been on criticism and tests, it might feel strange to give compliments. Even if you feel like you are complimenting others too much, you probably aren't.

Hint: Compliments are also a great way to ask for a favor. Adjust the level of flattery as needed – too much brown-nosing can be counterproductive. For example: "Hey Laura, you've got a great eye for product design and really pay attention to the details that make a difference. Would you mind jotting down a few ideas on what you think I should change for the new software? Your input would really mean a lot to me – I don't know anyone else that can do what you do." Can Laura really say no to that?

Hint: Taking a compliment isn't easy either. Don't belittle what you're being complimented for. "Oh I just threw a few ideas together," "anyone could have done it" or "it was nothing" are counterproductive. You're indirectly criticizing the judgement of the person giving you the compliment, making them less likely to compliment you in the future. Go for a "thank you, I'm glad you like it" (or something similar) and smile instead. Remember what compliments you received so that you can pick up on them when discussing promotions or salary increases

108. Find your ideal sleep cycle and wakeup time.

Waking up at the end of deep-sleep phase will leave you well-rested and ready for a day at the office. To find your personal deep-sleep cycle:

- Record when you went to sleep, when you woke up, and how you felt during the workday.
- Set your alarm clock 15 and 30 minutes earlier. Combine this with going to sleep 15 and 30 minutes earlier. Record how you feel in the morning.
- After two weeks of experimenting, you can use your records to find your ideal sleep cycle.

Hint: Avoid electronic devices about 30 minutes before going to sleep and (at least) for the first 10 minutes after waking up to improve how well you sleep or feel after waking up.
Hint: According to research, your sleep cycles are approximately 90 minutes long. That means you should sleep multiples of 90 minutes – i.e. 6, 7.5 or 9 hours.

109. Learn to fall asleep in 2 minutes.

The US military spent a lot of money researching how to get their soldiers to fall asleep quickly and avoid fatigue-based mistakes. The resulting technique described below is said to work for 96 per cent of people after six weeks of practice (so don't give up after only a few weeks).

- Relax your face muscles, including your tongue, jaw and the muscles around your eyes.

- Drop your shoulders as far down as they'll go, followed by your upper and lower arms, one side at a time.

- Breathe out, relaxing your chest followed by your legs (starting from the thighs and working down to your toes).

- Spend 10 seconds trying to clear your mind. Then focus on one of the three following thoughts:
  You're lying in a canoe on a calm lake with nothing but a clear blue sky above you.
  You're lying in a black velvet hammock in a pitch-black room.
  Mentally say "don't think, don't think, don't think" to yourself over and over.

110. Learn to "meal prep."

Not buying a coffee every day at work adds up. Skipping that 5 US$ daily coffee for 220 days a year (and drinking the office coffee instead) translates to over 1,100 US$ that you can spend on other things instead.
Not buying lunch every day adds up even more. Google or search for YouTube videos on how to meal prep. There are really great (and healthy) recipes out there.

111. Adjust your work based on personality types.

There are a lot of different frameworks for categorizing people out there. One of the most famous is the "Hartman Personality Profile" which groups everyone into one of four "personality colors". Get familiar with the characteristics of each color and learn to adjust your interactions and work to each of their personality colors. For example: If your boss has a "red" personality, focus on the vision/big-picture, hard/logical facts, and concrete actions – don't focus on emotions. If your customer has "yellow" personality traits, focus on making your product/service sound fun to them and be emotional and enthusiastic about it.

112. Use your own products.

If you're not using your own product, what business do you have expecting others to buy or use it? By using your own product, you are better able to understand its strengths and weaknesses. Such insights are invaluable when deciding on new additions or tweaks to your products. You're also sending the clear message (inside the company and to the general public) that you are proud of and trust your product.

113. 1-3 goods points are better than 10.

When trying to convince colleagues of your idea, you may be tempted to write a long "laundry list" of all the different benefits. Writing such a list will mix the strong and important benefits of your suggestion with the weak and less important benefits. These weak points become targets and cause doubts to arise about the other benefits you listed. Try to focus on a maximum of three benefits which your audience can easily remember and recite.

114. Make the most out of business trips.

Travelling for work does not always have to be a chore. Use the advice below to make the most out of your trips:

- **Maximize loyalty points.** Make sure you are earning points for every night spent in a hotel, every flight taken and every car rented. Check out which loyalty programs there are and then book your travel to maximize the loyalty points earned. Be aware that there is usually a company policy as to the maximum you can spend for business travel.

- **Book in advance and then cancel flexibly.** If you travel regularly and want to maximize your points, you should always have a room booked for the next 7 weeks. Booking in advance ensures you have a room during trade shows or citywide events – and continue collecting loyalty points. Be sure to check the airline's or hotel's cancellation policy and then set yourself a weekly reminder in Outlook to check whether or not to cancel next week's reservation.

- **Add a day or two.** If you are travelling close to the weekend, you can try to add a day or two to explore the city you are in. If your company allows you to fly earlier or later, then you can have a mini-vacation and only have to cover the costs for the extra hotel night(s).

- **Plan buffer times.** Don't miss your train or flight because of a traffic light cycle or a difficult customer in front of you. Planning in some extra time makes travelling much more relaxing.

- **Buy a sticker for your check-in baggage.** Search on eBay for "fragile" or "priority" stickers and buy those that most resemble your airline's stickers. They may not be official but they do work, as luggage handlers don't have the time to inspect the authenticity of each sticker.

- **Pick the right waiting line.** Avoid lines with older people or families with kids. Look for the line with experienced travelers with laptop bags and small carry-on luggage. If you have the option of going right or left after a ticket check or security check, always go left. Most people go to the right which means longer waiting lines.

- **Invest in a good eye mask or neck pillow for power napping.** Block out the generous lighting on those early flights or trains and arrive well rested instead of red-eyed.

- **Wear comfortable clothes on long flights.** Long flights will leave a suit wrinkled. Wear sneakers, comfortable pants and a hoodie instead. Then change into your suit at the hotel. Wearing a crisp, unwrinkled suit will make you look fresh and ready-for-business.

- **Be friendly from the get-go.** Whether talking to the receptionists, taxi drivers or housekeeping staff — first impressions count. Always remember that the people you are being friendly to can make your business travel more pleasant. Especially if you regularly travel to the same city and use the same airlines/hotels.

- **Ask for the room you want.** After staying in the same hotel for a while, you get to know which rooms are quieter or closer to the elevators. Ask for them when checking in.

- **Hang your shirts and suits near the shower.** Take your business clothes out of your suitcase as soon as you enter the room. Use coat hangers and let gravity do the work. If you hang your clothes near the shower, the steam helps reduce wrinkles.

- **Take care of your health.** Travelling can be demanding and stressful. Choose hotels with fitness facilities and block some time to actually use them. The same goes for taking the time to rest and get enough sleep.

- **Store some stuff at the hotel.** If you are visiting the same city often, you can ask the hotel to store a bag of yours. Into this bag, you can put toothbrush, toothpaste, and other amenities, as well as your sport shoes and an extra charger or so. That allows you to travel more lightly.

- **Reception has spare chargers.** If you have lost or forgotten your mobile phone or laptop charger, you can borrow one at the reception. They usually have spare ones or a box full of chargers other guests have left behind.

- **Fill out the feedback forms.** If employees have gone the extra mile, help them get their good work recognized (and get them promoted).

- **Don't forget your business cards.** Travelling usually involves meeting new people. Introducing yourself without a business card looks unprofessional. The likelihood of that person ever contacting you also drops significantly, since they don't have anything to remember you or your contact details by.

115. Avoid rush hour traffic.

Ask if you can come in (and leave) an hour later to avoid peak traffic times. If you can't avoid traffic, try finding gyms or other hobby/sport/academic courses nearby – better to spend an hour after work there than in traffic.

Hint: If you are stuck in traffic, use comedy podcasts to heighten your mood or audiobooks to pass the time. Some colleagues even learn new languages while commuting.

***

116. Try exercising before work.

Contrary to what you may think, working out before starting your day actually increases your energy at work. It also increases your metabolism so that you burn more calories throughout the entire day.

Hint: Studies have shown that attractive people are rated as being better at their work and are even promoted more. Getting a good exercise routine may actually help you earn more in the long run. Think about it – who would you trust more at work? The healthy, energetic person or the slightly obese, constantly yawning coffee-addict?

***

117. Look busy – always.

Keep a folder, some papers or a notebook under your arm when walking around your office. With these simple props, even a casual stroll to the snack machine looks work-related.

You can also look busy by covering your desk or office wall in complex-looking printouts. Just make sure you can say something intelligent about the printouts in case you get asked about them. Be sure to change the printouts regularly – having the same graphs tacked to your wall ruins the impression of looking busy.

This hack of always looking busy enhances your reputation as a highly engaged and valuable employee. As an added benefit, looking busy means that no one will suspect you of slacking off (even if you sometimes are ☺).

✷ ✷ ✷

118. Walk with purpose.

Walk quickly and look slightly irritated or stressed – even if you are just walking to the coffee machine or the toilet. Having such an expression on your face makes you look busy and will dissuade people from burdening you with additional tasks. Look around at the executives in your office; they will typically be walking with purpose.
Hint: Depending on your company culture, this hack may backfire. If your bosses make it a point to be approachable or relaxed, your busy appearance may be counterproductive.

✷ ✷ ✷

119. Create a slide collection if you use PowerPoint a lot.

If your job involves creating a lot of PowerPoint slides, create a new file called "Good Slides.pptx". Having such a collection of good slides will save you a lot of time on future PowerPoint presentations.
Hint: Add good slides from colleagues to your collection as well. You can also add good slides from other companies – just make sure to adapt them a little so that you don't accidentally plagiarize.

✷ ✷ ✷

120. Collect good emails.

Whether it is an inspirational email from leadership or a well-written happy birthday email, save these emails and use them for inspiration when you need to write your own. This also applies to introductory emails from new employees or farewell emails from soon-to-be ex-employees.

121. Use inspiring names.

Give your ideas, projects or initiatives interesting, attractive and distinct names. This will make marketing your ideas within your company a lot easier. Convincing others to join you or provide you with resources also becomes easier. Which of the following projects sounds better? "Interface Update 2.0", "Digital Sales Booster" or "Moonshot"?

122. Learn persuasion.

There are several magic words and concepts which can help you persuade bosses, colleagues and customers. If your job involves sales, you should buy yourself a few books on persuasion.

- **Pace your audience**. Tell your audience what you want them to think – pace their thoughts. For example, before telling your listeners about your innovative idea, tell them "What you're going to see next is how we reach the next million customers." You have just paced your audience – they will now be evaluating your idea with the thought you just implanted in their heads ("this is how we get the next million customers").
  You can also pace your audience by prefacing a controversial idea of yours with "At first glance, my idea may seem radical, but the more you think about it, the more attractive it becomes." Your audience will

(involuntarily) focus their energy on trying to find out how your idea seems attractive.

- **Use magic persuasion words**. A magic word to use is "imagine." You force your listener to very actively envision your idea and embellish it with whatever is most important to them. The vaguer your phrasing is, the more room your listener has to imagine/fill in the details. For example, Hillary Clinton asked potential voters to "imagine a dark presidency under Trump" – the word "dark" being one which nearly everyone can interpret differently.
Other words with a highly positive association are also highly persuasive. Try to work in "new," "free," "instant," "easy" or similar words into your concept.

- **Add a "because"**. Adding a reason makes it easier for your audience to rationalize why they should agree with your suggestion. Try to have a good, logically sound "because" reason. If you don't have a good reason, even a bad reason is better than none. According to a famous study, 93% of people let someone cut in line for a photo-copying machine when asked "Can I cut in line for the photocopier because I need to make a copy?" The "because" reason used in the above example is nonsensical; of course you need a photo-copier to make a copy.

- **Use numbers**. Why do all the clickbait articles on the internet have titles such as "10 things to improve your sleep" or "20 things you need to know about raising children"? Because it works. So, add a few numbers to your message – just make sure they are written as numbers (i.e. 7 instead of seven).

- **Repeat, repeat, repeat.** The more often you hear or see something, the more you'll tend to like and accept it – also known in psychology as the mere exposure or familiarity effect. Repeating the same message (using the same words) in your presentations will increase its persuasiveness.

    Your message will also be more persuasive if your audience hears it from other people than yourself. So, take the time to tell your boss' colleagues, employees, and assistants about your new idea. By the time you present your idea, your boss will have heard about it already (hopefully multiple times). As an added benefit, hearing the same message from multiple people gives it what psychologists call "social proof" (i.e. if everyone is talking about it, then it must be good).

- **Be visual.** Your idea will be more persuasive if you can make your listeners visualize what you are saying. These highly visual phrases can be both positive (e.g. piles of cash) or negative (e.g. train wreck).

- **Contrast.** Most advertisements use comparisons (before vs. after or our product vs. our competitors' products) because they work. Contrasting your ideas can be both positive ("our pricing is better than 90% of our competitors") or negative ("without this change, our company loses hundreds of customers").

- **Wording matters.** Don't use double negatives ("I don't think we shouldn't do that"). Also, keep your message as simple as possible. For example, the slogan of AVIS (the number 2 car rental company in the US) is "We try harder."

Or that of Disneyland is "the happiest place on Earth." Both are short, simple, and to the point.

123. Provide the illusion of choice.

Bosses, colleagues and customers typically prefer to choose from between different options. Use this pop-psychology knowledge to provide your boss with several options and present the option you prefer as the highly favorable. This "illusion of choice" will make your boss feel as if they had made the decision themselves and increase their buy-in. Instead of saying your project will cost 6 million dollars, present three options costing 3 million, 6 million and 9 million respectively. As if by magic, everyone will agree that the 6 million option is the best choice.

124. Go "past the sale."

A clever negotiating trick is to make the other party think "past the sale" and focus on aspects beyond the yes or no decision. Car salesmen often ask you whether you would prefer the car in silver or red – they don't ask you whether you like a car at all. Some exemplary uses of this "hack" in your office are:

- "Do you have time today or tomorrow?" instead of "When could we meet?"
- "Are the costs-saving or quality improvements of our software more important to you?" instead of "Do you want to buy our software?"
- "Which of these starting dates for our project do you prefer?" instead of "Can we do this project?"

Hint: A very powerful question to ask is "How can we make this work?". If used after a suggestion you made, the listener or reader focuses, not on whether your suggestion make sense ("should we?), but on the changes that need to be made in order to implement your suggestion ("how can we?").

✶ ✶ ✶

125. Write during meetings.

Always write something down during meetings. Not only does this help you remember what was said during meetings, it also makes you look organized and helps you stand out. After a while, you will be the go-to person if someone forgets what was said during a meeting.

Avoid falling into the trap of becoming the "office scribe" – i.e. being invited to meetings only to record what was said and not having any active role. This often happens to junior employees when more senior employees don't want to transcribe the meeting themselves. If you feel that you are becoming the "office scribe," schedule meetings (with a friendly colleague) which coincidentally conflict with the meetings you are being asked to transcribe. After a few schedule conflicts, some other poor soul will have become the new "office scribe".

Hint: If you're stuck in a nonsensical meeting, write down your shopping list, your weekend plans, or ideas for your friend's birthday present. To an unknowing onlooker, you look like you're studiously taking meeting notes.

If someone asks you to share your notes and all you have is a shopping list, you can always say you were only writing down points important to yourself or (if the meeting was a while ago) that you threw out your notes during one of your regular workspace-cleaning sessions.

***

126. Learn to draw.

The adage "a picture is worth a thousand words" also applies to office work. Convincing others of the merit of your ideas is much easier if can visualize your new idea for an improved shop layout, a better production process or re-organization of customer support. Workshops or meetings also become a lot easier if you can quickly sketch your thoughts (or someone else's).
Hint: Even if you're not a talented artist, you can still master the basics by practicing. There are courses offered by online universities or tutorial videos on YouTube. An easy approach is to do a Google image search for "hand drawn business icons," print them out, and practice one icon every day. By combining simple shapes and icons, you will soon be able to visualize nearly anything.

***

127. Dress to impress.

There is an old saying which says to "dress for the job you want, not the job you have". Be intentionally stylish with your office attire and aim for dressing 10-20% better than your peers. If you dress sharply, you'll stand out and people will think you're more competent (similar to the psychological "halo effect").
Hint: For inspiration, you can use Google image results for "stylish office wear," fashion magazines, or look at what leaders in your company or industry are wearing. Just don't go overboard and overdress – it will make you seem egotistical and superficial.
Hint: You can always try to wear something unique which will make you stand out – think of the iconic black shirt & jeans combo that Steve Jobs wore. You don't have to go that far

though — just wear glasses with a thick, red frame or some brightly colored socks (now nearly mainstream in investment banking).

128. Look professional when VIPs visit.

You never know when an important customer or the CEO decides to visit. Keep a comb, some hair gel and deodorant or mints close to you. A spare tie or business shirt is a good idea if you're prone to eating messily and staining your work clothes.
Hint: Keep your spare clothes in a dark place. Otherwise they'll get bleached by the sun.

129. Bring candy to difficult meetings.

When we eat candy, our brains are flooded with the neurotransmitter dopamine — putting us in a better, more agreeable mood. No one is immune to this physiological reflex. If you expect a meeting to be difficult because of office politics, cultural differences or diverging opinions, a little bit of candy can make a huge difference. This is especially so if some participants skipped breakfast, already had several back-to-back meetings prior to yours, or your meeting is a very long one. You will be amazed at how candy can help reduce the tension or facilitate the reaching of a consensus or agreement.
Hint: Bring one or several large containers of mixed candy — they are easier to transport, increase the odds of everyone finding a flavor they like, and look better than having lots of sweets scattered around a table.

130. Always thank people.

Always thank people when they helped you, no matter how trivial their help was or whether it would have been part of their job anyways. The people you thanked will remember that you appreciated them and be more willing to help you should you require their help again.

Hint: Even better than thanking a coworker is telling their boss what a good job they did. Your compliment may have a positive impact on your coworker's annual performance review, which greatly increases their likelihood to help you again.

131. Do "rounds".

Try to regularly talk to everyone in your office, even if just to say hello. Find common interests or topics which enable running dialogues that you can easily pick up on to make small talk. Adjust how much you talk based on the personality of your colleague – for some people a simple nod is all the small talk they need.

Doing such "rounds" will help you if you need a small favor. The regular interaction makes a "yes" much more likely. You won't be considered as someone who only interacts with others when you want something.

132. Find a routine outside of work.

Find a hobby, sport or side project that you pursue outside of work. Not only will a healthy work-life balance make you a more interesting person, it will also give you something to look forward to while at work.

133. Keep a book related to your job on your desk.

Always have a book which is relevant to your position lying openly on your desk — be it about project management, IT skills or market trends. You can read it and further educate yourself during work hours or use it as a prop to make yourself look like an engaged, smart employee. If you just want to look smart, buy secondhand books (they are a lot cheaper and look used).

✱✱✱

134. Keep track of contacts.

Add new contact details to your phone or Outlook address book as soon as possible, especially if you have hundreds or even thousands of contacts. An up-to-date overview of your contacts means never wondering who is calling or being unable to selectively ignore certain callers. You don't want to be losing new or important customers by not identifying their calls as VIP enough to leave a parallel meeting or conference call.

✱✱✱

135. Keep track of birthdays.

Schedule Outlook reminders for the birthdays of important colleagues or customers. A birthday greeting is always a good occasion to refresh your relationship. After congratulating, you can usually slip in a few business-related questions. A phone call is better as it's more intimate and dynamic than an email. If you do send your greetings via email, write a birthday greeting which you can quickly personalize to save time.
Hint: Christmas and other holiday greetings are also a perfect occasion to catch up. Even though not everyone may reply or even like getting greeting cards, 99% of recipients will appreciate the good-natured gesture.

136. Keep spare birthday cards.

Keep a few spare cards for congratulating colleagues on birthdays, marriages, births or promotions. That way, if you forget or just found out about a friendly or very important colleague's birthday, marriage, etc., you can quickly write a congratulatory card. A card has a much more personal touch than an email. Getting colleagues to sign can also add a nice touch.

137. Smile more.

Not only does smiling release endorphins and improve your mood, it is also contagious. Try to find a routine at work where you have something to smile about. I start my days off with a Dilbert comic.
Hint: If you have nothing to smile about and are working from home, you can just hold a pencil (lengthwise; horizontally) between your teeth. This pop-psychology trick activates the same muscles as smiling and has been scientifically proven to put you in a better mood. Just don't do it in public; you will get strange looks and colleagues won't lend you their pencils anymore.

***

138. Take notes digitally.

Try to go a day without taking handwritten notes, and then slowly work your way up. Taking notes digitally has a few major advantages. Digital notes can be easily organized and are completely searchable. They can also be forwarded or submitted for feedback with a simple click. That means no more searching

for past notes or trying to decipher what you wrote last year.
Hint: You can take notes using OneNote, MS Teams or any other collaboration software. Alternatively, you can write your notes directly in Word documents or emails. Some touchscreen laptops or tablets enable you to write notes with a digital pen. These handwritten notes are then automatically converted to searchable text.

GETTING YOUR BOSS TO PROMOTE YOU

Your boss is probably too busy to dedicate enough time and attention to each individual employee. As such, it is up to you to stand out from the rest of your colleagues and get your boss to promote you. With these simple hacks, you can accelerate your way towards higher salaries by gaining your boss's respect and trust!

139. Network in your industry.

Your boss will be impressed if key people in your industry know you by name. Even better is if you can personally introduce your boss to people in your network. A good network will also make you a more valuable employee and make you more prone to receiving attractive job offers.
Here are a few hacks to help you quickly network:

- Google your industry and use search terms like "market trends," "key developments," "top speakers," "expert," "guru," "leader" and so on. Find the people listed as authors or leaders and write them an email or connect with them via LinkedIn.

- Search for industry associations, groups or organizations. Check if your company is a member or would pay for your membership. Upon joining, write introductory emails to other members or (more effectively) write the organization's management and ask if they can introduce you to people relevant to whatever you're working on. You can also offer to help organize events or take on an official role (treasurer, editor etc.) to boost your network.

- Attend industry conventions and trade fairs. Such in-person events are perfect for networking and meeting people from competitors as well as (potential) customers and others from academia, government and related industries.

- Find out which journals and magazines as well as analysts from banks or research firms cover your industry. Reach out and network with the reporters and analysts – both groups are usually well connected. Be sure to not give any interviews or provide sensitive information without getting a written OK from your company first.

- Network with academics, research institutes, think tanks or government bodies that are active in your industry.

- Volunteer for career fairs and other recruiting events. Since companies in the same industry typically are interested in the same employees, you can use such events to get to know employees from other companies.

- Start writing articles for industry magazines and on LinkedIn. Be sure to engage with people who comment on your articles on LinkedIn and also comment on others' articles. Each time you write, you are increasing your industry prominence and contributing to expanding your network.

- Join internet platforms like meetup.com or reddit.com and find groups related to your industry.

140. Use Google Alerts.

Set Google Alerts for your boss's name and their boss's name, your company name and the name of your most important customers and competitors. That way you are always up to date on any breaking news. To learn how, just Google "how to set up Google alerts"

✦✦✦

141. Share information.

If you happen to know something relevant to your boss's work (i.e. something about their customers, new trends, competitors), then share it with them. A quick email is enough ("FYI, did you know that …" or "FYI, thought this might be relevant to your work on …"). The worst thing that can happen is a reply with "Thanks for the heads up, I found out yesterday".
Hint: Share often, not just before annual compensation discussions. The more often you get your boss's (positive!) attention, the better.
Hint: This also goes for sharing information with colleagues. If you can save a colleague a few hours of work or provide them with a new insight before their next meeting, they will be more likely to reciprocate with a favor someday.

✦✦✦

142. Google important people in your company.

Google your boss and your boss's boss. Chances are you will find a profile, an interview or even presentations or speeches they gave. Use these sources to find out more about their past and opinions as well as what would impress them. Then, when talking to said important person, casually bring up some of their viewpoints or use some of their phrases. If you don't make it too obvious that you are "trying too hard" or simply parroting phrases without having thought about them, said important person will be glad to have found someone who "speaks their language." It's simple psychology.

143. Know what your company is doing.

Read the annual or quarterly reports or press releases to see what your CEO or company is telling the public. By knowing what your company is doing, you can impress your boss by showing an understanding of how your activities fit into the bigger picture of the overall company strategy.

Hint: You should also know what KPIs your company uses to measure success. Does the CEO highlight the customer growth, customer satisfaction or the dollar spend per customer? What are the KPIs included in the reports for upper management? By knowing which KPIs really matter, you can focus your efforts on making these KPIs better and accelerate your career.

144. Focus on "the new."

Taking over an "old" task from a previous person means you will always be compared to your predecessor. It also means you can't bring in your own ideas or change the "old" task too much without potentially upsetting your predecessor.

The trick is to be responsible for something "new" — a new technology, new customer, new product or new process. That way, you can quickly make a name for yourself and not have to compete with someone who has decades of experience.

145. Use professional jargon.

You'll find jargon in documents from your boss, your boss's boss, as well as other influential internal company players and external industry analysts or leaders. Using such jargon will make you sound like management material. You'd be surprised how much more attention your opinion gets if you start adding buzzwords like customer-centric, growth hacking, value strategy, diversification effort, multi-year planning etc. Just don't overdo it.

146. Adapt to your boss.

You can score points by adapting to the mannerisms, principles and expressions of your boss. If they like to read meeting documents at least a few days before the actual meeting, get used to sending them relevant documents a few days prior. If your boss believes in honest criticism and expects everyone to say their opinion, be bold and share your honest opinion. If they use specific expressions such as "growth booster," "efficiency driver" or "excellence" often, you can't go wrong with using them as well.

147. Ask for feedback frequently (and act on it).

Adjusting your work to your boss's preference is much easier with frequent feedback. Smaller, incremental adjustments are a lot less stressful than surprise last-minute changes or unpleasant accusations such as "I wish you'd asked me earlier." The more occasions you give your boss to voice his or her thoughts, the better you can tailor your work and the less wiggle room they have to complain.

A lot of managers say that employees stop asking for feedback after the first few weeks or months on the job. Frequently asking for feedback is a good way to get more face-time with your boss and an insight into how he thinks (what does he like, what is important to him when evaluating others etc.). It also demonstrates your high motivation and lets you know whether you're still on track or not.

Hint: Do you want to be promoted in the next 12 months? Do you want to improve on your presentation skills? In order to make feedback more effective, think about what your goals are and discuss them with your boss. After discussing them with your boss, write down your goals and record your feedback in order to track your progress over a longer period of time. This record of your goals and received feedback is a very useful foundation for annual performance review discussions.

148. Proofread your work.

This really isn't so much a hack as it is a prerequisite for being taken seriously. After all, how important can your work be if you can't even write down your thoughts correctly?

Proofreading is especially important if your work will be seen by your boss (or boss's bosses) or made public (press releases, marketing materials etc.).

Hint: Take a short break between completing an assignment and proofreading it. If you are consistently having trouble with proofreading, find someone in the office and ask them to help you out. Just be sure to act on their feedback – they won't be helping you for long if you make the same mistakes over and over again.

149. Always know what you're working on.

If your boss asks you what you're doing, you should be able to quickly rattle off all of the things you're doing (ideally in order of priority). Your boss will probably leave you alone to do your work instead of having to spend time re-prioritizing your tasks.

This hack works especially well for micro-managing bosses who get a warm, fuzzy feeling when seeing that you are on top of things.

When reciting the list of what you're doing, think of it as a mini-sales pitch in which you are trying to make yourself sound like a highly productive (and promotable) employee who is constantly adding value to the company. Saying "I need to write that white paper" is not impressive. Better to go with something along the lines of "I am currently researching how to win over airline companies and make the first million dollar sales. I already found some really insightful information so far but think that we need a bit more beef to make this paper a real trailblazer [and so on]".

✱ ✱ ✱

150. Keep track of what you did for performance reviews.

Keep a running list of tasks you worked on, especially those which were a personal favor to your boss or went above and beyond your work description. Use this list as a basis for any discussions related to salary increases or performance reviews. You will find that your boss will have forgotten most of the tasks on your list. The more you remind them of the value you added and results you realized, the better for your career.

✱ ✱ ✱

151. Regularly CC your boss when they are away.

Send your boss a few emails which show how busy you are while they are away on business or vacation. Such emails show them that you can work independently and reliably, even in their absence. And that is exactly the kind of reputation you want when it's salary negotiation or promotion time.

152. Update your boss before & after holidays.

Before you go on holiday, create a list of the topics you are working on, their current status, and the next steps. Use this list to update your boss so that he feels like you are on top of everything and doesn't need to get stressed while you are away on some faraway beach.

Make a similar list for when your boss returns from his holiday, so that he knows (and appreciates) everything you have been doing.

153. Reply quickly – especially to your boss.

People get a good feeling about you if your reply to voicemails or emails quickly, it makes you seem on top of things. Your reply doesn't have to be a solution or an answer – simply acknowledging an email or giving an estimate as to when you can work on it is more than enough.

You can set up an Outlook rule to highlight emails from your boss or other VIPs or move them into a separate inbox folder. Just Google "Outlook rule to highlight emails by sender" or "Outlook rule to move emails by sender" respectively.

154. Don't surprise your boss.

Your boss is expected to know what each member of their team is working on. Surprising your boss publically – even with good news – makes them look uninformed. Be sure to keep your boss up to date. It can be as easy as a 10-word email.

155. Impress your boss's boss.

Your career will benefit each time you are able to make your boss look good in front of their bosses.
It's easy: Find out who your boss's boss is. Then praise your boss in front of their bosses. This praise can be anything from an email ("FYI, [boss] and I won the Stanley account") to sharing a success story in a meeting, to an intranet or LinkedIn post. Find out what your boss's boss is most likely to notice and tailor your approach.
The key here is to not make the flattery too obvious or meaningless. Try to make the compliment about your boss casual or relate it to a topic currently relevant to your boss' boss (strategy, culture, customer satisfaction etc.). Here is an example of flattery I recently overhead: "Hi [boss's boss name], great talk yesterday about the importance of selling as a team. Did you hear about [your boss' name] new weekly "team sales planning" initiative? It may be something that other departments want to copy."

156. If you believe in something, just do it.

Sometimes you see a large opportunity but your workday is already full. In that case, invest time outside of work into this side project. Don't wait to be asked or assigned. Don't wait for the long decision-finding processes. Show some initiative and just do it. It can do wonders for your career.

As an example: A colleague thought digital marketing could improve sales. Unfortunately, no one else thought digital marketing was important. He spent his evenings learning about digital sales and created a detailed digital marketing strategy together with mock-up advertisements. After presenting the case, he got the go-ahead and was promoted to global head of digital marketing. If he hadn't invested some of his own time, he would not have been promoted.

Hint: Pick a side project where, if you fail, there's no (financial or reputational) damage to you or your company. Also pick a side project which interests you or where you learn a new skill. That way, the costs of failing are low, but the potential upside for you and the company is very high.

★★★

157. Organize company events.

Help your boss with organizing department offsites, office parties, trade conventions or similar events. You will benefit from an additional chance to prove yourself in front of your boss, while they will be grateful for your help. Provided the event is a memorable success, you should see a positive impact on your career.

Hint: Adjust the event agenda to your boss's personality. Very often, bosses like to hold speeches, give awards or use the occasion to meet a celebrity speaker or musician. Should your boss's boss be at the event, adjust the event agenda accordingly. Your boss will be happy if you impress their boss.

Hint: Regularly update your boss about how the planning and organization is going. This increases your exposure to your boss while giving you the chance to take into account their personal preferences early on (thereby avoiding unpleasant surprises). Don't go overboard though – you don't want to be spamming your boss about every single detail.

Hint: Get someone to take photographs so that the event becomes more memorable. An easy hack to get people to take pictures is to set up a photo booth with costumes (funny glasses, wigs etc.) or empty picture frames (a standard at most weddings nowadays). After the event, you can send people the pictures (or have a photo printer there), which provides people with a nice souvenir of the event you planned.

Hint: If catering is involved, be sure to ask attendees if they have any allergies or food preferences. Attendees who can't eat any of the food at your event are sure to be unhappy attendees.

✶✶✶

158. Give small gifts.

Bosses are people too. As such, they also like to celebrate their birthdays, successes at work or other holidays like Christmas. A small token gift or card will do – just make sure that your gift is in good taste and is appropriate price-wise. Go for something around 10-25 US$, which is the equivalent of inviting your boss out for lunch and covers the price of most good books. You don't want to send the message "here is a gift, you'd better promote me or else."

Hint: A good gift is a book about trends in your industry. Adding a personal inscription really helps your gift stand out.

Hint: A few other good gift ideas are a small plant, coffee or tea blends, or personalized pens or coffee cups. You can Google "gift ideas for bosses" for ideas. Aim for gifts that have a personal touch. Although it is the proverbial thought that counts, a gift which shows that you really thought about your boss's personal preferences counts a lot more than a dull, uninspired gift. If you are good at drawing, painting, sculpting or photography, you can give your boss something you made yourself. A painting, a tastefully sculptured coffee cup or a framed picture of the office complex or your team are all good ideas too.

COVERING YOUR ASS (CYA)

CYA hacks can save your career when someone is looking for a scapegoat or you have to justify your behavior. "Covering Your Ass" can also be useful for documenting inappropriate behavior in your office or getting leverage to ensure that you survive the next round of cuts. Think of CYA as an insurance policy – you don't want to be without it when you need it!

159. Show what (or who) is hindering progress at work.

A successful career depends on a lot of different factors – most of which are outside your direct control. In order to cover your ass (CYA), you should regularly and very explicitly show what (or who) is holding you back.

Use as many status reports, emails or face-to-face meetings as necessary. Be very explicit/direct in your phrasing. Euphemisms or overtly optimistic projections help no one. You should strive to give your boss or colleagues as many opportunities as possible to step in and help you. Nonchalantly saying that you have a problem and then waiting a few weeks will not absolve you of responsibility.

Hint: You should always inform people BEFORE you start showing others that they are holding you up. It is only fair to give them a warning and a chance to react. If you feel the need, you can always put more people on CC so that there is more pressure on the delinquent individual.

Example 1: "Dear John, our Indian colleagues need the complete product specifications by this Friday. Any specification not included will not be provided – there are no exceptions. I am meeting the IT-head tomorrow at 11:00 and need to know if you can meet our Friday deadline. Please confirm that you can make this deadline."

Example 2: "Dear Jane, attached is a draft of our weekly status report. I have set our overall project status to red since we are missing your input regarding the product specifications. I have to submit the weekly status report by Wednesday 12:00 and wanted to let you know first about our changing the project status to red. Do you think we can solve the product requirements issue? Please let me know by 10:00 tomorrow at the latest. Thank you."

160. Backup CYA-Emails.

Did your boss ask you to falsify financial data? Did HR write that you need to fire Arnold because he is just too old and smells funny? Does the new software update documentation confirm that cars' CO_2 emissions are being illegally falsified?

Having a backup copy of such emails is always a good idea. Especially if you have been locked out of your company's IT systems and are in the midst of litigation (i.e. suing or being sued). That is why it is critical to backup CYA-Emails <u>first</u> and then talk to your HR department or get legal advice.

To CYA, just send a copy of such emails to your private email account, ideally as a ".msg" attachment (simply drag the email from your inbox into an empty email to attach it as an ".msg" file). You can also BCC your private email address when replying to "critical" emails. "Critical" means all emails which are inappropriate or with a questionable ethical, legal or moral content.

Hint: Save copies of incriminating emails as ".msg" files. These ".msg" files are near unchangeable and therefore much better evidence. Forwarding emails is not as reliable, as the text of forwarded emails can be changed or original emails (on company servers) deleted.

✯ ✯ ✯

161. Get requests for questionable tasks in writing.

Savvy colleagues will ask you to do something shady or unethical over a coffee or over the phone – that's because they don't want anything in writing which can be traced back to them. What you need to do is to write a CYA-email after the informal coffee or phone call. This CYA-email should document whatever they told you to do and ask them to confirm whether you understood that correctly ("Did I understand correctly that you asked me to ...?"). Such CYA-emails are also a good litmus test – if you get a written reply, chances are that their request was not highly unethical or illegal.

If you don't get a reply or only get a reply over the phone or in person, you should again write a CYA-email. In this second CYA-email (ideally with the first CYA-mail attached), thank them for confirming your understanding during the phone call or in-person meeting and ask a follow-up question (e.g. "When do you want me to start ...?", "Does Mr. ABC know about this ...?", "Who else on the team should I inform about this ...?"). If you again only get an oral reply, then write a third CYA-email saying you don't feel comfortable and would like to get an OK or second opinion from your boss, colleague etc. Such CYA-emails make it clear to the other party that you are not an easy victim. Don't be hesitant to write such CYA-emails. Imagine facing jail time for having (unwittingly!) helped Bernie Madoff defraud his investors. A simple CYA-email can mean the difference between jail and freedom.

Hint: You can also use CYA-emails to pin down colleagues who are pathological liars or drama queens. Write down and ask them to confirm every single task and instruction. Once you start doing this, there will be a lot less of "I never said that," "you did it completely wrong" and "why did you go against my instructions". After a few times of playing this game, the pathological liars and drama queens respect that you know how to CYA and adjust their behavior.

162. Get any harassment in writing.

If co-workers or bosses are bullying you or discriminating against you, try to get it in writing. If you plan to raise the abuse with HR or even sue your employer later on, this written evidence will really help your case.

Hint: If you are thinking of suing your employer, then make sure you have already raised the issue with HR or with your boss. In most jurisdictions, the employer is only liable if they didn't do anything to stop the harassment (i.e. only after being made aware of it). Also get legal advice before suing – losing a coin-toss or being asked to re-fill the coffee pot is not a case of discrimination.

Hint: If the harassment is of a non-written nature (e.g. verbal or even physical abuse), goad your tormenter into providing you with written evidence. Your email should include a short description of what they did, how you don't condone such behavior and end with a provocative question (which will hopefully provoke a response from your tormenter, thereby confirming his negative behavior). Example: "Hey John, you called me a dumb blonde at today's review meeting. I've told you multiple times that I find this insulting and asked you to stop. Do you get enjoyment out of it?".

Hint: Send emails to other people who witnessed the workplace harassment and ask them for confirmation. Even if you don't get a reply from your tormentor, corroborating accounts with other witnesses is a good idea.

Hint: If you are consistently being harassed or bullied at work, keep a journal to record all instances. Such a record can show that the harassment was regular and not just a one-off exception.

* * *

163. Learn about memorandums and affidavits.

Memorandums and affidavits are written accounts of an event and can serve as a more formal document when you need to CYA. In cases where you have been discriminated against or abused, you may want to write an email to yourself containing your memories of the event. As all emails contain the time and date they were sent, an email to yourself can be a good form of documentation. The required formats and standards required to be admissible as legal evidence vary by country. If you are thinking about litigation, you should discuss your plans with a lawyer or at the very least do a quick Google search.

* * *

164. A diary never hurt anyone.

Presidents and other high-profile figures in public or private offices keep diaries. Such a diary can also make all the difference if you need to remember "what really happened" on a certain day, years afterwards – which is typically the case whenever lawyers are involved (e.g. insider trading, funds mismanagement, product recalls, fraud etc.).

Writing down your thoughts and reasons for taking certain actions or decisions on a regular basis can help you refresh your memory as to why you acted the way you did and what your available information was at the time. Companies downplaying the harmful side effects of medicines, purposely deceiving investors, or paying bribes, are (unfortunately) more common than one may think. A lot of involved (innocent) people regret not having kept a record or diary or some sort.

Hint: Don't tell anyone at the office about your diary. Although you may only have the best intentions in mind, colleagues may view you in a different light.

Hint: If you want to use your diary as a legally valid document, check with a local lawyer or notary. A quick-fix to "prove" that you wrote a diary entry on a certain date is to send yourself a copy of your diary via email (either a scan of your handwritten notes or the digital text itself). Since the time and date of an email sent to yourself cannot be altered, such emails can help you avoid allegations that you "doctored" your diary later on – which can play a vital role in litigation or proving your innocence to the wider public or media.

Hint: Definitely keep a diary if you are working in a role which may be of interest to the public or plan on becoming a whistleblower. In that case, you can use your diary to quickly write an autobiography and retire early.

165. Use your smartphone camera & microphone.

If you can't get something in writing, try and get an audio, photo or video evidence using your smartphone. Depending on your local legal system, smartphone evidence may not stand up in court. Nonetheless, most companies will be willing to settle outside of court in order to prevent embarrassing scenes from being made public.

✶✶✶

166. Use disclaimers for your work.

You never know to whom your work may be forwarded to. There is a lot of potential for misunderstandings – e.g. preliminary estimates being understood as final calculations, ongoing discussions being read as final outcomes or confidential data being made public.

Add disclaimers to your emails and work documents to be on the safe side and CYA. For emails, add the disclaimer in red, bold text at the very top. For documents, add a prominent disclaimer as a watermark or on the header or footer of every page. Exemplary disclaimers you can use are "preliminary figures," "first estimates," "for discussion," "not yet reviewed," "OK from legal pending," "draft version," "strictly confidential" or any combination thereof. Your key objective is to ensure that you are in the clear if someone misunderstands your work.

✶✶✶

167. Give ranges for numbers.

If you are unsure about providing a quantitative estimate or calculating a business case, you can use ranges to CYA. The chances of your figures being wrong sink proportionally to the size of your range used. A range of +/-10% is completely normal, with larger ranges acceptable for more uncertain figures.

168. Learn weasel.

There are certain "weasel phrases" which can be used unethically. "Some say," "most people think," "evidence suggests," "researchers believe," "it has been said that," it is regarded as" are all "weasel phrases" that can be misused to make your idea seem more accepted.
Another example is saying "my understanding was ..." instead of "I assumed". This puts the onus on the other party to prove that they communicated correctly.

169. Offer a reward for lost items.

Write down your personal contact details in your notebook or laptop and offer a reward for their return. With a laptop, you can put your information on your login screen.
Adding your personal contact details and a small reward prevents your lost items from being sent directly to your company. You thereby reduce the likelihood of getting disciplined for carelessness with confidential data or the loss of company equipment.

170. Don't cheat on travel expenses.

One of the first areas that HR looks into when your company needs to downsize or fire you is to see if you submitted any suspicious expenses. Expensing that Saturday night taxi ride to the bar is not worth it. If your company has previously fired people for cheating on their travel expenses, photograph potentially suspicious receipts next to a note stating the reasons why you expensed it. That way you have covered your ass if any (mistaken) accusations as to your honesty with expensing arise – which can sometimes happen years later.

OPTIMIZING YOUR WORKSPACE & STAYING HEALTHY

Governments are constantly increasing the age at which you can finally retire. Why not make your workspace as comfortable as possible while also maximizing you chances of being healthy enough to enjoy your golden years? The hacks below help you improve your workspace and your health at work!

171. Stop slouching.

Regularly check whether your desk, monitor, chair etc. are positioned so that you aren't slouching. Eight hours of bad posture per day will soon leave you looking like the hunchback of Notre-Dame and with back pains.
This hack was mentioned multiple times as an absolute imperative by old-timer office veterans. Even the most expensive (and painful) back surgeries cannot undo decades of bad posture.

172. Find the correct screen and keyboard position.

A simple rule is to sit back in your chair slightly reclined (at an angle of 100-110°) and hold your right arm out horizontally. Your middle finger should almost touch the center of the screen (monitors should generally be at least an arm's length away from you). From this position, you can then make minor changes to the screen inclination and height.

If you regularly have neck pains or a stiff neck, then you're possibly tilting your head forwards because your monitor is too low. If you have shoulder pains, you're probably tilting your head backwards because screen is too high.

There are lots of tutorials on YouTube on the ideal way to sit or stand at work

Hint: If you use a laptop, you can either buy laptop stands, a separate screen, or just use some books to position the screen until it is at eye level. Also recommended are an external mouse and keyboard.

173. Use F.lux.

At justgetflux.com, you can download F.lux, a free program which automatically adjusts the color of your computer screen according to the time of day. When the sun rises, your screen is adjusted to the sunlight outside – when the sun sets, your screen is adjusted to your indoor lighting. This significantly reduces the strain on your eyes.

Hint: You can also buy glasses with a blue filter to use in the evening. These glasses reduce the negative effects screen time has on the production of sleep-inducing melatonin.

174. Get a good chair.

Seriously, get a decent chair. Your back will thank you. Ideally, get your company to cover the costs fully or at least meet you somewhere in the middle. If your boss complains that it isn't a good investment, remind them of the fact that a good chair lowers the risk of long-term carpal tunnel and back injuries, which means fewer sick days. Sitting comfortably also means you can spend more time working and less time being distracted or in discomfort due to a cheap chair.

175. Get two screens.

Working with two screens will significantly increase your productivity, especially if you need to compare two documents or read input from an email while using a different program. If you have never used a dual screen setup before, you cannot imagine how beneficial this change can be.

176. Get an ergonomic keyboard & mouse.

Ask HR or your boss if you can get a vertical mouse and an ergonomic keyboard which is curved and more suited to the human body. You will be able to work/type faster and greatly reduce the risk of long-term injuries such as carpal tunnel syndrome.
Hint: If your office doesn't want to pay for a new keyboard or mouse, offer to split the price. Even if you have to pay for everything yourself, it's still a worthwhile investment – just ask any orthopedic doctor for their hourly rates.

177. Get a "sit-stand" table.

Get a table where you can change the height to either sit or stand when working. People who only sit at work have a statistically significant lower life expectancy and are at a higher risk of back injuries and even hemorrhoids.

178. Get a screen privacy filter.

A privacy filter enables only those sitting or standing directly in front of a screen to see what is being shown on that particular screen. Anyone "shoulder-surfing" or trying to sneak a peek will see only a black screen.

No matter if you want to keep your work confidential or play games on social media while at work, a privacy filter can save your job. No need to let the entire office see your intimate vacation pictures or the latest restructuring plans exclusively entrusted to you.

Hint: Good filters cost quite a bit – try to get your employer to cover the costs. If you work in a large open office or have your back to a window (corporate espionage can be as simple as a camera and a telescopic lens), keeping your work confidential is a legitimate business concern.

179. Get plants.

It has been scientifically proven that plants not only improve the air quality, but also cheer you up. Go to a local garden store and ask for advice on which plants are best suited to your climate. Some plants require little care and no sunlight, others are more high maintenance.

180. Get comfortable shoes.

You may want to think about keeping an extra comfortable pair of sports shoes or slippers in your drawer. Business shoes have thin soles, tough heels and are usually not recommendable from an orthopedic perspective. Should your boss or an important customer come along, you can easily switch back to your business shoes. If your role allows you to always wear comfortable shoes, you should banish your uncomfortable business shoes to a bottom drawer.

181. Don't keep stuff in your back pocket.

If you have to sit for many hours a day, having something in your back pocket can shift your balance and slowly but surely lead to bad posture or back injuries.

182. Exercise your lower back.

The human body was not made to sit for hours at a time. One of the areas that is most affected by sitting is the lower back. Start doing daily lower back exercises or exercises that work the core. YouTube is full of 5-minute videos which make a huge difference in the long run and are still doable in an office setting.
Hint: If you feel self-conscious about exercising at your desk, book a meeting room or use the printer or office supply room. You can also ask a colleague to join you.

183. Remember to get up and move around regularly.

If you are digitally inclined, you can set up regular reminders to "get up and move" in Outlook. Getting up and moving around a bit has been proven in multiple studies to reduce the negative long-term health effects of office work and also free up your cognitive capabilities.
If you aren't digitally inclined, use a small glass for staying hydrated. Each empty glass is an easy reminder to get up and move around more often. Alternatively, you can place items you

use often (trashcan, binders, staplers etc.) as far away as possible from your desk. Each time you need to use said items, you are forced to get up and move around.

Such small changes may not seem like much, but adjustments to your daily routines can quickly add up.

Hint: If you're self-conscious about walking around your office aimlessly, get some smartphone headphones. To an onlooker, you seem to be taking a call or participating in a conference call.

Hint: Placing items further away is also useful for unhealthy snacks. According to pop-psychology, the further away you put a snack, the less likely you are to eat it (a locked drawer several meters away from you is ideal).

***

184. Eat & sleep healthily.

To be physically able to enjoy retirement, you need to eat healthy and get those 7-8 hours of sleep every night. Not only will you be in better shape, you'll also find that work is more pleasant if you aren't sleep-deprived, obese, or running on empty calories.

Focusing on both sleep and nutrition prevents a negative feedback loops. If you sleep badly, you're more likely to eat junk food; if you eat junk food, you're more likely to sleep badly. Ad infinitum.

***

185. Keep pictures on your table.

Keep pictures of your family/partner/friends/pets on your desk. Such pictures can raise your spirits and help you through stressful times, especially if you remind yourself that your work is helping to pay for your child's ballet classes or football practice. If you're a more materialistic person, you can put a picture of your next vacation destination or the car you are saving up for. You can of course also add such pictures to your computer's desktop background.

Hint: If you don't like pictures on your desk, a souvenir will also do the trick. It can be something as simple as a pebble from your honeymoon resort or a paper boat your son made you for father's day. Important only is that you associate fond memories with the souvenir and can relish them if office work gets too hectic.

186. Deck out on office supplies.

Keep highlighters, whiteboard markers, post-it notes and other useful office supplies on your desk. Even if you don't use them, they will make you look like a real hands-on person. Even better, colleagues may come to you to borrow them from time to time and make you look like the go-to person in the office.

187. Keep a stash of "happy food."

Everyone has a favorite food or drink which can immediately raise their spirits. Keep a small stash hidden in one of your drawers for when you need a small "pick me up" to carry you through a really rough day. Just make sure it is something like candy, dried fruits or nuts – otherwise your stash may spoil and you will have accidentally created a small mold kingdom in your drawer.

Hint: As tempting as it may seem, alcohol is not a good idea. If someone finds out, you will have an unshakeable reputation as a functioning alcoholic.

188. Have a backup meal.

Sometimes you or a colleague may have to stay a bit later or work through lunch. Keep a "backup meal" that is somewhat healthy and has a long shelf-life – think canned foods, instant noodles or similar. It's not ideal, but it definitely beats going hungry or replacing a meal with candy bars.

189. Create a small "office apothecary."

Think about creating a small "office apothecary." Just the basics of aspirin, paracetamol or ibuprofen and cough drops can make a huge difference. You don't want to be without it if you're stuck in the office and not feeling your best.
Hint: Depending on where you live, you may be liable if you give your colleague some medicine and they suffer an adverse reaction. Google your local laws to avoid well-meant but costly and embarrassing situations.
Hint: If you are really sick, go home. Being sick and in the office can infect other colleagues, causing them to be sick. Studies have shown that the positive contribution made by attending work when sick is vastly overshadowed by the risk of your illness taking out other colleagues.

***

190. Avoid offices next to meeting rooms.

Do you want endless unwanted visitors asking for directions to the meeting rooms? Do you enjoy hearing the small talk of meeting participants prior to and after each meeting? Do you like to return to your office and have to search for your chair after it has been borrowed for a meeting? I rest my case.

If you work close to a meeting room with glass walls, you can kiss your privacy goodbye. Bored meeting participants will be constantly trying to see what is on your computer screen (which is why you should get a screen privacy filter).

Hint: Offices near hallways should also be avoided as they get a lot more visitors stopping by. You will also be distracted by hearing random snippets of conversations from people walking past your office.

Hint: Offices with a closed door, where you are sitting opposite the door, are the best. Such offices allow you to work with fewer interruptions and also give you a few crucial seconds to close any non-work-related windows on your computer. If you have a large window behind you, check to see if your computer screen is reflected in it.

UNETHICAL HACKS

When interviewing "office veterans" for this book, a lot of them shared unethical hacks which they would like the next generation of office workers to (ab)use. Your employer (or legal system) may not be very happy with you using these hacks so (ab)use them at your own risk!

191. Successfully fake being sick.

Over 40% of employees fake being sick to take a day off. If you are taking fake sick days very often, it is a sign that you are unhappy at work and should seriously think about changing employers. Listed below is the best advice on how to fake being sick successfully.

- **Think of your colleagues.** Your time off work affects your colleagues. Be considerate of their workloads before choosing to fake being sick.
  Hint: A better solution than taking a whole day off may be to come in for the first part of the day and then leave. Take care of urgent matters and be quiet. If anyone asks what's up, just say you don't feel well. When you decide to leave, simply tell your boss that you're sick and going home for the rest of the day – tell them, don't ask. Explain that you've taken care of all the urgent work for the day and there is no way your boss can say no.

- **Choose a good date.** Taking a Monday or Friday off makes it seem like you want to extend you weekend. Go for the days in the middle of the week instead. That way you can also set the scene the day before.
  Hint: The perfect time to fake being sick is if you have been sick for a couple days already but are feeling well. You can always claim you needed an extra day to be on the safe side and your colleagues will already have adjusted to your absence.

- **Don't tell colleagues.** The more people know, the higher the risk of someone accidentally exposing you as a faker.

- **Set the scene the day before.** It looks a little suspicious if you're energetic one day and suddenly sick the next. Pretend to be feeling under the weather the day <u>before</u> you plan on taking a day off. Don't be too obvious about it and try to fake cough. Just act a little bit under the weather – talk a little softer or slower, don't laugh or make as many jokes, and dampen your usual enthusiasm or energy. Publicly take a harmless vitamin pill or two that resembles an Advil or aspirin. Turn down invitations to lunch or happy hours the day before you call in sick. Ask colleagues for a cough drop or other over-the-counter medicine such as ibuprofen (don't take it).

- **Call in sick early.** Set your alarm between 4 and 5 in the morning and send a short email along the lines of "feeling sick and didn't get much sleep, will try to come in later today if I can." Then shut off your phone and pretend you slept all day.
  A second option is to call your boss right after waking up at your usual time – your raspy voice and your tiredness will

make you sound sick on the phone. Calling early also increases the likelihood of reaching your boss's voicemail or catching your boss when they are off guard. Calling too late makes you look less responsible and attentive of your boss.

If you call in sick, call your boss directly. Otherwise you may have to fake everything all over again in another call!

- **Keep emails or texts brief**. If it's an email, just write "Feeling sick. Staying home today" in the subject line so that your boss has already accepted the information before reading any of the email's content. In the email body, don't write anything more except that you'll try to come in later if you feel better. If there is a critical piece of work or meeting your boss need to know about, write a short sentence on what to do. Don't elaborate on what sickness you have or on any symptoms – a brief email makes it seem like you really are struggling. In most countries, your employer is not allowed to call out your bullshit story by law, so creating an elaborate cover story is not worth the effort or risk.

  If it's a text, the same goes. Keep it brief along the lines of "Hi Diane, I'm not feeling well. Will let you know if I feel better and can come into the office later on." To appear sick, take longer than usual to reply to texts and reduce the number of emojis used.

  Hint: If you really want to make a good impression, say that you'll do your best to come to work later on or the next day and that you're grateful that your boss understands. Pretend to be sad about missing work and show how eager you are to return to your responsibilities – without overdoing it! This will make your boss feel like you're genuinely sorry to take a day off instead of wanting to take a day off.

- **Avoid social media.** Posting pictures and writing hundreds of comments is not something someone sick would do.

- **Choose the correct illness.** To miss one day, you should go with food poisoning or a migraine. To miss multiple days you should go with menstrual pains, eye infections or (most common) a flu or cold. An upset stomach is one of the best illnesses to use since it has no visible symptoms and is a bit disgusting (i.e. people won't ask you about it). On your first day back, you have to eat some dry bread, bananas or something similarly bland to fake your return to health.

    Hint: If someone in your office was just genuinely sick a few days ago, claim to have the same illness as them. That is easily believable since you could have caught it from them. Claiming to have the same sickness as a colleague also provides you another reason to stay at home – you want to prevent other colleagues from catching the same contagious sickness you yourself caught.

    Claiming to have caught a sickness from someone else (it could also be someone outside of work) is a good idea. That way, your boss can't request you return to work since they would be jeopardizing the health of other employees. In the post COVID-19 era, such a request could be career-destroying.

    Hint: Be sure to know some of the symptoms of whatever sickness you claim to have. Food sickness, for example, typically takes about six hours to manifest and is usually caused by fish or mayonnaise. If you complain of a migraine, only one specific area of your head should hurt and most light and sounds should bother you.

- **Shop around for a doctor's note.** If your company requires a doctor's note, call different doctors and ask what their policy is. Tell the doctor that a note is formally required by your company, but you're typically not the type of person who shows a lot of symptoms even if sick. Rather than facing a potential malpractice lawsuit, most doctors will write you a sick note (even if they suspect you are only faking being sick). I personally witnessed a doctor giving out sick notes for not having slept enough and feeling "too tired" for work. Try out multiple doctors and find the one that is lenient. If you know a doctor or have a doctor in your family, then you can typically ask them as well. Just don't use a doctor with the same surname as yourself since this can arouse suspicion.
When getting a doctor's note, ask for an "excused from work" date further away than you really need. Then you can go back to work "early" and look like a dedicated employee who uses less sick time than necessary. Returning "early" also reduces the chances of your sick days being questioned in the future.

- **Fake symptoms, if you must.** If for some reason you do have to make a call while pretending to be sick, you can still fake a few symptoms. To fake a sick voice, lie on your bed and have your head hang over the edge while breathing only through the mouth and not taking deep breaths. To fake a sneeze, inhale a tiny bit of pepper or pluck a few nostril hairs with tweezers, then look at a bright light. To fake a cough, try to eat a small teaspoon of ground cinnamon.

- **Play the part the next day.** Don't return into work looking perfectly healthy. Pretend to still be returning to health. Openly take a few vitamins, blow your nose a few times or cough softly. Don't play it up too much – just don't sound as though you just returned from a relaxing day off.
Hint: Be extra nice to your boss for the next few days after returning. Remind them of what a valuable and loyal employee you are to remove any doubt they may have as to the authenticity of your sickness.

192. Write vague requests if you need a lot of help.

This hack relies on the psychological underpinnings of the "foot-in-the-door" effect. If you need a significant amount of input or help, the best hack is to be deliberately vague about how much help you need in your first email or phone call (i.e. get your foot in the proverbial door). Once the other party has agreed to help you based on your vague request, you can then spell out exactly what you need. Had you immediately asked for a large favor, they may have ignored or declined your request.

193. Be as vague as possible about deadlines for yourself.

Bosses and companies love clear-cut answers to the "by when can you do that?" question. You want to avoid committing yourself to a specific date – there are too many external factors which may influence your ability to hold a deadline. A sick colleague, a computer crashing, a boss who tells you to prioritize something else – the list of factors is near endless.

The trick here is to be as vague as possible while still begin definite. Saying you'll finish a project in February or in the first quarter of 2020 sounds definite and reliable, but leaves you a lot more leeway compared to committing yourself to the 14th of February 2020.

Hint: For smaller tasks where external factors play less of a role, a very precise deadline can be beneficial. For example, if a colleague needs a file from you, say that you'll send it over by three o'clock. By having committed to such a specific time, you'll be more motivated to do the small task. If you forget, your colleague will have a clear deadline after which they can send a gentle reminder.

194. Set your out-of-office-message in advance.

This hack will save you from last minute work. Colleagues who get an out-of-office-message (OOM) from you will automatically assume that you are unavailable, even if you're still in the office. If you're going to be gone for a few days, set your OOM at the start of your last day at work. If you're going to be gone for a week or two, set your OOM a day or two prior to leaving.

Just write something along the lines of "Thank you for your email. Please be advised that I will be unavailable from the [future start date] to the [end date]. I will reply to your email as soon as possible upon returning".

Hint: You can also extend your OOM to include your first day back. That way you won't be invited to meetings and can spend your first day getting rid of the emails you received during your absence.

195. Always be busy or away on chat software.

If your company uses something like Skype, set your profile to "busy" or "away" to save countless hours of time. Your status also allows you to reply at your own leisure, as colleagues wait patiently for you to return or finish whatever was keeping you busy. If your profile is set to "online" or "available," colleagues expect immediate replies and can take delayed replies as a personal insult or sign of general laziness.
Hint: Setting your profile to "busy" is the better option, as your boss gets the impression that you're constantly working (and not just "away").

196. Tactically schedule your emails.

Every email of yours can be configured to be sent at any time in the future – it doesn't matter if it's a minute, an hour, a day, a week or even a decade from now. That means that even though you clicked send, that email will be in your outbox until it is sent at your pre-defined date and time.
Scheduling an email to be sent late at night, early in the morning or on weekends makes you look like a hard worker – even if you are in bed and sleeping at the very moment your email is sent. You can also schedule emails to be sent later if you finished a piece of work, but want to pretend that it took a bit longer. Google "How to delay or schedule sending email" to learn how to schedule your emails.
Hint: Don't send emails outside of work hours if your company has a strict "no work outside of work hours" policy. Don't use this hack of sending emails late at night or on weekends if your job is easily doable – it looks like you aren't being productive enough during office hours

***

197. Write or read at work.

If you're bored at work and have nothing to do, start writing a novel in your email program. To a passerby, it looks as if you are writing an email.

Alternatively, download eBooks as PDF documents and convert them to word documents (just Google "convert pdf to word online free"). To a passerby, it looks as though you were reading a market report instead of the latest bestseller.

198. Use proxies to access blocked sites.

Some websites are probably blocked in the office. If you Google "free online proxies," you can access these blocked sites. Just be aware that you should not use these proxies for anything confidential or requiring a login as you don't know if your data is transmitted securely. Alternatively, you can use your smartphone to surf around; just be aware that surfing via smartphone makes you look less busy.

Hint: If Facebook or other social media websites are blocked at your workplace, you may want to think about using a premium proxy service (i.e. it will cost you a few dollars a month but your data will be more secure).

Hint: Make friends with the IT team to learn what websites are blocked. If you have a good enough reason, you can always request that access be unblocked.

199. Cultivate a reputation for being a little unreliable.

A reputation for being slightly unreliable or sloppy can be beneficial (assuming you aren't pursuing a salary increase or promotion anytime soon). Colleagues will stop asking you to do extra work and lower their expectations as to the quality your work – making your workday much easier and freeing up a lot of your time.

Hint: If you don't want a bad reputation, you can also avoid extra work by being someone who asks a lot of questions when given a task. If you ask enough questions when given a new task, whoever asked you to do the work will at some point realize that it is quicker to do it themselves. In addition to asking questions, you can also constantly ask for input or feedback while working on the task – this shifts the responsibility back to the person who asked for your help.

✶✶✶

200. Photograph good excuses.

Have you suffered a flat tire or cracked windshield? Was your house broken into or damaged in a flood? If so, take a picture and use it as a really good excuse for work absences, missed deadlines or late replies.

Hint: You could theoretically use any picture from the internet, but a simple reverse-picture-search can reveal whether that picture is your own or not. You could also take a picture of a random flat tire or cracked windshield but it won't work if the car color or make doesn't match your own.

Hint: Be sure to delete the metadata of a picture so that a tech-savvy boss can't immediately check on what day the picture was taken. To learn how, Google "delete picture metadata."

✶✶✶

201. Use phone calls to leave early.

This hack works best if you can get your girlfriend, boyfriend or partner in on it. You leave work early by loudly exclaiming (while on the phone) that you will need to continue working when you get home. After all, who would dare penalize you for leaving work early when you have just said that you will be working from home?

Some employees have taken this hack too far and pretended to be on the phone, only to receive a call midway through their act. If you think you have the acting skills to pull it off, ensure your smartphone is in flight mode.

202. Leave early by using spare jacket or keys.

Leave a spare jacket on your office chair when you go home. To any passerby, it will look like you are still in the building.

A keychain with some keys casually left on your desk adds to this effect. You can buy used keys at flea markets, locksmiths or online.

A less environmentally friendly alternative is to leave your computer and lights on when you leave.

203. Arrive a little early, leave a lot earlier.

If you are regularly bored at your desk with nothing to do for the rest of the day, this hack is for you

Arrive at the office 10-15 minutes before everyone else and make it look as if you have already been there for a long time (i.e. don't be taking off your jacket or booting your PC when your first colleague arrives). Your colleagues will have no idea what time you arrived, allowing you to leave the office much earlier. Just be sure to reference (loudly and often) that you put in the hours by coming in earlier. If you're asked when exactly you arrived you can always give nonspecific answers like "how early I come in depends on how much I have to do."

Hint: In order to avoid being caught out, you need to make sure that no one logs your attendance (through CCTV, parking badge logging or computer-usage tracking). If your job doesn't require you to use your computer, you can always say you were preparing for the day using printouts etc.

* * *

204. Bring snacks if you're late.

If you overslept, buy some treats for the office or meeting. Colleagues will dismiss your lateness as being due to your having stopped at a donut shop or bakery. Additionally, they won't care about your lateness as much once they're eating a muffin or donut.

If you don't have a good reason for why you brought treats, say that you just felt like it. No one will press you on whether or not your reason for bringing treats is legitimate.

Hint: If you bring snacks "just because," then wait until 10:00-10:30 before bringing them out. Your colleagues will already have finished their most urgent emails and are starting to get hungry. That makes them more likely to stop by for a snack.

* * *

205. Close your office door sometimes.

Keep your door open when you're really working, allowing any passerby to see how busy you are. Close your door and ask people to knock whenever you're in meetings or on calls. After a while of following this pattern, you can close the door anytime you want to slack off. Everyone will have gotten used to knocking first, giving you a precious few seconds to stop slacking and regain composure.

***

206. Get an "I'm busy" sign.

If you have colleagues who are a bit too chatty, think about getting a small sign with "do not disturb," "on a call" or "out to lunch" etc. You can usually find professional-looking signs like the one shown below on eBay or Amazon. You can easily personalize the signs with a simple color printer.

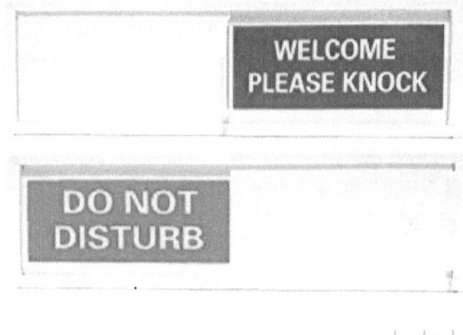

***

207. Get a mechanical keyboard.

If your job involves typing a lot and you aren't in a large open office, you may want to think about getting a mechanical keyboard. People walking past will hear you typing a lot and assume you're hard at work – even if you're just writing a Facebook comment or a shopping list.

Hint: Mechanical keyboards create noise and can be very annoying to your colleagues. Ask them beforehand.

***

208. Get a Rubik's cube.

A Rubik's cube or similar puzzle will allow you to get many breaks from work while also making you look intelligent. No one will really care if you waste hours on it as it doesn't arouse suspicion and makes you look smart.

209. Don't return on Monday.

Whether from vacation or after maternity or sick leave, don't ever go back on a Monday. That is the day when most work gets allocated. Aim for returning on a Wednesday or Thursday. Starting with a shorter workweek also makes returning to work a lot easier.

210. Drink what others are drinking.

If you are someone who likes to drink a lot on company outings, don't go for exotic drinks. Drink what everyone else is drinking. It is much better for your drinks to blend in with the rest when the bill arrives.
Hint: Don't drink too much if you can't handle yourself. Your colleagues will remember your behavior and you may say things that come back to haunt you.

211. Keep important documents.

Don't delete or throw away everything related to your old job once you change employers. Be sure to keep important employment contracts or other documents which you may need to Cover Your Ass someday.
As an example: A structural engineer had warned his company

multiple times that a bridge was not safe. When the bridge collapsed 11 years later and his old company tried to drag him into it, the documents he had archived exonerated him and saved him a lot of legal costs (and even prison time)!

Hint: Some companies or legal systems forbid you to take documents with you, as they are confidential or company property. Check with a lawyer or you may be sued.

LEADERSHIP HACKS

Every company is constantly talking about leadership. Leadership is all about building, inspiring and continuously optimizing a high-performing team. Everyone has their own leadership style – these hacks will hopefully make leading your own team a bit easier!

212. Show how and why it's done, don't do it yourself.

As a leader, your job is to ensure your team knows exactly what to do. Create daily or weekly meetings where you go through questions the team has. Then take the time to show how and why it's done. Each time you do so, you enable your team to become more independent. Explaining the why improves the decision-making capabilities of your team.
Avoid the temptation of doing it yourself – you deprive your team of valuable experiences. Even if it may be quicker or better that way, you will be frustrated and eventually overworked. A minute invested in teaching your team saves you five later on.
Hint: Depending on how large your team is, you can also call everyone together on an ad-hoc basis.

213. Try to accommodate families and lifestyles.

In some cases, offering flexible work hours or schedules can be a bigger motivator than promotions or salary increases. Parents who can start earlier, get to pick up their kids from school or help their kids practice for a dance recital are more likely to work hard

to keep that privilege. They are also less likely to switch to a company without such an accommodating work schedule.
The same principle also works with people who are devoted practitioners of a sport or hobby. Freeing up the schedule of a dog-enthusiast employee in order for them to attend the national finals with their dogs will win you their loyalty.
Hint: Depending on your industry and function, relaxing the dress code can also have a positive effect on morale. Just be sure to communicate that while dress codes may be relaxed, expectations regarding work results aren't.

214. Try out results-based leadership.

If you can set your team clear goals, you can give your team more flexibility on how to reach them. Once they have completed their goals, they can go home or spend their time as they wish.
This results-based approach often motivates employees to get results as quickly as possible. Just be sure that you also define standards regarding quality or methods so that you don't get results which are unsuitable.

215. Try letting your team self-select.

Write out all the different tasks that need to be done by your team. Hold a meeting and ask your team to complete the list. Then invite your team to self-select what they would like to do. Ask your team members to choose based on what interests them – not what they have already been doing for years. Enabling your team to self-select increases motivation and instills a stronger sense of ownership.

Hint: You will have to step in if multiple people want to do the same task. Ask each team member to elaborate on why they want to do the task. Then suggest that after a certain time (e.g., 6 months) they can switch tasks, or ask for one of them to concede (if necessary, throw in a "goodie" to make the concession easier). If no one wants to do the task, then you can highlight why that task is interesting (i.e. make it sound more attractive) or throw in a "goodie" to motivate someone to volunteer.

216. Try letting your team define your role.

If you are given a new project team or department to lead, try out something new. Get your team together and ask them two simple questions:

- At the end of our project, when we are successful, what will you say that I did?

- At the end of our project, if we fail, what will you say that I did?

Give your team a day or two to think about their answers. Then call your team together to collect and jointly review all the answers given. Using the input from this workshop, write the job description for your role. Send this description to your team and ask them to approve the final version in a short workshop.
Hint: You should also ask your team to think about how they will evaluate how well you are doing and how to provide you with feedback on your performance.

217. Take the time to know each team member.

Take the time for one-on-one meetings. Find out what each person's goals are, what motivates them and what they don't enjoy. Encourage them to talk about what is on their mind and about their life outside of work.
Having a close, personal bond with your team enables you to be a better leader and to get the best out of each team member.
Hint: Coffees or lunches are ideal for catching up and less formal than meetings.

218. Synchronize your team.

Have team meetings at least once a week. These meetings don't have to be long – they can even be just 15 minutes a day. The objective is to synchronize your team, i.e. discuss the week ahead as well as the previous week.

219. Appreciate your team.

Go out of your way to thank people for what they did. This works wonders as your team will be more motivated and perform better.
Hint: Try to make it more than a "thanks." Take the time to highlight what your team member did and why you appreciate it. Ideally over a coffee.
Hint: Praising team members publicly is also very effective. Give people credit for their ideas and accomplishments in a meeting or at a team event; whether or not to call for a round of applause is up to you. Sharing credit publicly not only doesn't diminish your standing, it improves it because people admire and

appreciate the ability to give credit. As the saying goes, "Praise in public, criticize in private."

★★★

220. Use the PPPF framework for one-on-ones.

One-on-one meetings are important for leaders to touch base with their team and stay on top of things. Unfortunately, these one-on-ones often become redundant or don't have enough clear actionable results. Tell your employees that your one-on-one meetings are based on the PPPF framework:

- **Private:** Is there anything in your private life you would like to share? If it's something positive (e.g. pregnancy), I want to congratulate you. If it's something negative (divorce), I will try to take it into account regarding work.

- **Plans:** What are your plans until our next one-on-one? The more I know about what you are doing next, the better I can try to help you or connect you with another employee relevant to your plans.

- **Progress:** What progress have you made since we last spoke?

- **Fires:** Are there any pressing issues I should know about?

★★★

221. Build your team to be complementary.

Create a team where the strengths and weaknesses of each individual complement each other. If your super creative marketing employee is not able to keep track of marketing spend, pair them with someone highly analytical – allowing each individual to utilize their respective strengths.
Hint: You can involve your team – list all the activities your

department is responsible for and then hold a meeting where each team member can say what their strengths are and which activity they would like to do. This exercise will make obvious what "gaps" you need to fill and what complementary skills you need.

✶✶✶

222. Promote a healthy work-life balance in your team.

As tempting as it may be to be available 24/7 during vacation or drag yourself into the office even when you're feeling sick, don't do it. Your employees will feel pressured to adopt your unhealthy approach. In the long run, your best employees will either burn out or leave your team or company.
Great results come from happy employees that are engaged at work and have sufficient time to refresh outside of work. You want to set a positive example for your team to follow. If an employee is feeling sick, send them home. If an employee replies to an email during their vacation, make it clear that you do not expect that of them.

✶✶✶

223. Promote a feedback culture.

Use meetings or one-on-ones to find out how you can enable your team and individual employees better. Encourage employees to proactively give you feedback. Show your appreciation when you receive feedback – e.g. by highlighting how you changed something based on feedback received and giving credit to the person who gave you the feedback.

✶✶✶

224. Rotate your team.

Employees continuously doing the same tasks become bored and develop a "tunnel vision." By rotating your employees into other positions within your department, your employees learn new skills, stay engaged and stay longer. Overall communication, cooperation and the levels of knowhow across your team will increase. Doesn't that sound good?

Hint: Rotating your employees with other departments in your company is also a good idea. Talk to the departments to the left and right of your part of the value chain and ask if you can send an employee for "work shadowing." By knowing what other departments are doing, your team will be better able to work together across company silos.

225. Stand behind your team.

As a leader, you are paid more money to take responsibility for your team. If someone on your team makes a mistake, shield them from blame. After all, it is your job to ensure that everyone on your team knows what to do and that they are doing it correctly. Taking the blame and standing behind your team will make your team incredibly loyal to you.

226. Get out of the office.

A leadership role typically means a nice office with a door. Don't get trapped into the habit of leaving your office only to attend meetings. If you don't get out of your office, you have to rely on secondhand evidence – i.e. the reports of employees who want to keep their job. Employees who want to keep their jobs are (understandably) likely to paint a rosier picture and unlikely to point out what the real problems are.

To remind yourself to get out of your office, block 2 hours a week or more in your calendar. Use that time to experience sales, logistics fulfilment or application processing firsthand. Walk the production floor, listen in on a few customer service calls or do some "work shadowing." That is the only way you can see what works (and doesn't work).

227. Ask "what's next?".

It's easy to get caught up in just "doing your job." If you focus too much on driving the train, you might not notice you're running out of track. And sooner or later, your train is going to derail.

In addition to excelling in their current role, leaders are expected to spend a lot of time thinking about and preparing for the future. As a leader, you should constantly be asking yourself "What's next?" – for you and for your company. Thinking about where you want to be in a year and five years from now increases your long-term chances of success.

Here are some "what's next" questions to get you started:

- What services or products will you provide a year from now? What about five years from now?
- Who will your customers be in a year? What about five years from now?
- What are relevant short-term and long-term trends?
- How will you differentiate yourself in the market? What are competitors doing and why?
- What skills and employees will you need?

- What other resources will you need?
- What long-term changes do you need to start today?

228. Learn story-telling.

Story-telling has become a leadership buzzword. Humans are biologically hardwired to like stories. Stories also inspire people much more than PowerPoint slides.
Here are a few tips regarding story-telling.

- Focus your story on <u>why.</u> Humans love knowing the detailed reasons for why something happened and don't care as much about what happened.
- Stories have a simple structure – a beginning, a climax and an end. Yours should too. In business situations, we often translate this into a situation, a complication and a solution.
- Start with a message or situation you can full-circle to at the end of your story. This will make your story more memorable.
- There has to be a protagonist or a few main characters (you, a colleague or a customer).
- You have to introduce your protagonist and flesh them out with some details.
- Mention the location. Don't ask why, but humans like to know where something took place.
- There has to be a problem or mystery. Humans love conflict and crave adversity. Ideally the problem gets

continuously worse – i.e. more interesting – during your speech.

- Humans like happy ends, so keep the lessons learned or morals of your story light.
- Use emotions and vivid, visual descriptions ("I felt ...", "I was horrified to hear that ...", "I couldn't sleep well that night, because of ...").
- Use the magic phrase "can you imagine how...?" phrase to propel your audience into putting themselves in your situation.
- Use breaks and pause for emphasis. Ask rhetorical questions ("What happened next?", "What do you think I did?" etc.) to keep your audience interested.
- Focus on positive messages and make your story funny. Avoid being a standup comedian.
- Use statistics and numbers sparingly.
- Use transitions to ensure your audience can follow your story ("a week later," "Because of my....," "Guess what happened next?").
- Practice, practice, practice. Steve Jobs supposedly practiced his Apple developer speeches for 2 full days.
- Deliberately focus your story on one key aspect and don't provide a detailed protocol of your entire life. Make the listener want to ask follow-up questions.

229. Learn how to ask for budgets.

To make things happen in an office, you need to be allocated a budget. This usually involves asking and convincing a lot of different people. Listed below are some tricks to make asking for budgets easier.

- First and foremost, find out who makes the decision on your budget. Find out what they are interested in and tailor your budget request accordingly. If you have to ask the IT-head for a budget, highlight the technology advantages of your idea or show that other leading technology companies are doing the same thing as you. If you have to ask the CFO, highlight the financial aspects such as increased revenues or reduced costs.

- Compare the budget you require to a very large number (other projects, market benchmarks, your entire company's revenues etc.) or divide it by the number of customers or employees that will benefit from it (e.g. this project costs only 2.5 US$ per customer).

- Break down your budget into tranches and only request the first tranche. By reducing the size of your requested budget, you have reduced the likelihood of being denied. Once you have gotten some money to start with, you will usually be able to get further tranches. Companies loathe cancelling running projects, especially when you highlight the costs required for ending and winding down your project if you don't get further resources.

- Show high, medium and low versions of your budget. These high and low versions of your budget are meant to be strawmen which make your medium budget seem reasonable. Make sure the high version of your budget includes lots of extra features and benefits which aren't essential. Make sure the low version of your budget does not yield valuable results.

230. Show the value-add of your department.

If you are leading a department, create an overview of what your department does and the value-add for your company. Aim to make your department look as valuable as possible to the overall company. Think of it as a marketing brochure which you can use when vying for budgets or onboarding new employees. A good overview of what your department does and how it adds value is also extremely useful when discussing your salary or promotion prospects. Involve your team for best results.

- Start by creating a list of all the services you provide. For example: If you are in charge of the controlling department, you could list the weekly, monthly and yearly reports your team regularly provides. You could also list the different type of ad-hoc analyses you provide other departments with. Lastly you could list projects your team is currently engaged in.

- In a new column, list how each activity helps and adds value to your company. For example: Your weekly sales controlling report helps efficiently allocate 10,000 sales staff in 10 countries and the spending of weekly marketing budgets totaling 3 million US$.

- In a further column, write who the beneficiaries are. In the above example of the weekly sales controlling report, it would be all sales and marketing departments for 10 countries.

- In a final column write which team members are responsible for the services you provide.

- On a new page, write down past achievements or awards. Did your team help reduce the financial consolidation costs by 100,000 USD per year? Did you create the sales dashboard for the new SUV your company produced? The more of a positive track record you can show, the better.

- Next comes the hard part. Use the information you wrote down to create a visually appealing and structured overview of what your department does. 3 to 5 pages should suffice.

Hint: If you are leading a project team, a marketable overview of your project is also a good idea. Make your project sound as important as possible, without bending the truth.

GENERAL POINTERS & MISCELLANEOUS HACKS

This book also includes pointers that are not hacks per se, but are nonetheless useful for your office work. Not wanting to deprive you of potentially useful ideas, miscellaneous hacks (which wouldn't fit neatly into any other category) are also included here.

231. Learn to small talk.

Small talk with customers or colleagues can be difficult. Observe others who are really good at it and see how they keep conversations positive, fluid and meaningful. One of the key success factors is asking questions and not making the small talk all about you.

If you're stuck for topics, just remember the acronym "F.O.R.D". The four F.O.R.D. topics listed below all have positive association and provide a lot of conversation material.

F = Family & friends
O = Occupation (i.e. their job)
R = Recreation (hobbies, sports, TV, books, holidays)
D = Dreams.

Hint: Avoid politics, religion and health as small talk topics. You can immediately poison a relationship by having an opinion which your counterpart considers "wrong."

232. Write effective LinkedIn connection requests.

LinkedIn can be useful for building a valuable network in your industry. Here is how to write a good connection request:

- **Click on the person's profile before clicking "connect".** This allows you to send a personal message along with your connection request. Otherwise your connection request is just the standard "I'd like to connect with you on LinkedIn."

- **See what you have in common.** Do you know them? Do you know someone in common? Do you know their company? Do you work in the same role or industry? Have you been to the same university or completed the same online course? Do you follow the same companies or are you in the same LinkedIn groups? Did you just attend their lecture or read their book? Use whatever commonalities you have to build rapport in your connection request.

- **Compliment them.** Write something positive about them or their company in your connection request. Everyone likes a little flattery – just don't go overboard or be disingenuous. See if you can relate it to something you have in common.

- **Explain why.** Write about why you want to connect with the person. Are you joining their company soon? Do you want to sell them something? Are you looking for someone to exchange ideas with? Or do you simply want to grow your network?

- **Be as informal as possible**. Did you already drink a beer together at the last convention? Or have you only read an article about the person in a trade publication? Whatever the case may be, try to be as informal as possible in order to make your business relationship a more personal. Don't be lewd or disrespectful; write as though you were writing to a friend. It will make your connection request seem warmer and less distant or impersonal.

- **Keep it short.** The more to the point, the better.

- **Add your contact details if you want them to contact you.** Make it as easy as possible for them to send you an email or call your number.

- **Follow up.** Build your relationship with your new connection. Send them an industry article they may find interesting. Comment on their posts. Ask them if they will be attending a trade fair. Write them if you will be visiting their city for business and ask if they want to do lunch. Invest some time and effort into building a long-term, personal relationship with LinkedIn connections that are important to you. If you can, try to meet in person. LinkedIn has made it easier than ever to connect with others, but face-to-face meetings still reign supreme when seeking to strengthen a business relationship.

Listed below are a few exemplary connection requests to help you write your own

- **Joining a new company/department**. Dear Elena, I will be joining your innovation lab next month. John told me about your role in the drone program – really impressive results! If you have the time, I would love to meet for a coffee or lunch. Looking forward to meeting you and the team! – Winston

- **Someone you met at a trade fair**: Hi Johnny, good to meet you at the CES in Las Vegas. Would love to discuss the airport analytics idea further. You can reach me at 0800 1234 1234. Best, Winston (P.S. Next time the beers are on me ☺)

- **Someone from the same industry**. Hi Roxan, I see you're also a member of the US Aerospace Engineering group. I'm very interested in hearing about what you (as lead design architect) think about the new journey to Mars idea. Let me know when you are in Dallas! Best regards, Winston

- **Someone you don't know at all**. Dear Markus, I just finished reading your "Digital Marketing 101" book and use it every day. Your marketing mix framework and advice on boosting performance marketing is extremely helpful to someone as new to the industry as me. I would love to connect with you to better follow your publications. Please write me if you are ever in New York – a coffee or beer of your choice is on me :-). Best regards, Winston (a fellow Penn State University graduate)

- **Someone you want to sell to.** Dear Amelia, I see you're the new HR manager at BMI – congratulations! I've worked with BMI on multiple HR initiatives in the past and would love to discuss how we can bring HR at BMI to the next level. The "strengths-based" leadership initiative at Snoogle or the cultural transformation at Snesla could be really interesting for you! Best regards, Winston (0800 1234 1234)

233. Stay hungry and don't become complacent.

Make it your number one priority to look out for your future and act in your best interests. Bosses notice if you've become too comfortable and mentally put you into the "passive office drone" category.

Continuously look for ways to leverage your skills and experience for advancement within your company as well as outside of it (including becoming an entrepreneur). Attend trainings or join teams where you can learn something new which makes you more valuable.

The secret to success is to become more valuable on company time (i.e. while getting paid). Find out which activities will benefit you the most. Then find reasons why your company should provide you with the necessary time and money to do them.

234. Have perspective.

No matter if you just accidentally messed up a critical presentation in front of investors, deleted your team's entire work or sent an embarrassing email to the whole company – disasters can and do happen in offices. No matter what happened, keep your cool. Remember that work isn't everything and that in a few years you'll probably laugh over whatever misfortune happened to you. It's only a job – people will soon forget and if not, there are always other places or ways to earn a living.

At the end of the day, you are just a number to your company. Companies exist to create value. Companies do not exist to be your friend and owe you no real loyalty beyond your paycheck. The second you quit, your company will try to replace you. What I am trying to say is that no job is worth losing family, friends or health over. There are more than enough jobs and employers out here. No one ever said "I wish I had spent more time at the office" on their deathbed. Keep that in mind if work stops being fun.

235. Avoid correcting others in public.

Unless you can do so gracefully and the mistake is important enough, don't correct someone else in public. This is especially true if you are in a meeting and want to correct your boss. Even though you may have the best of intentions, an ill-phrased correction can lead to resentment.

Instead, wait until a more private moment to point out the error for their reference.

Hint: Some companies have an "obligation to dissent" culture – i.e. you should always make yourself heard if you have a different, dissenting opinion. Depending on your company culture, correcting others (even in public) may be accepted or even required. This general pointer is more about corrections where your colleague risks losing face in front of others.

236. Talk up others.

Make it a habit to mention how well other colleagues are doing or how good their work is in public. It makes you look like a team player and as someone confident enough to promote others. As an added bonus, the person you talked up will usually find out about your kind words, earning you their favor. Just make sure that your positive comments are based on reality. Don't talk up someone who is very bad at what they do. You should also avoid talking up your direct competition for a promotion, otherwise you may get passed over.

* * *

237. Stay cool or stay at home.

No matter how angry or frustrated you are, don't lose your temper at work. It's always better to call in sick and stay at home to relax for a day than to freak out at work and get a bad reputation or problems with HR.

* * *

238. Think before spamming colleagues.

This pointer is all about respecting your colleagues' time. If you couldn't be bothered to invest some of your time, why should they invest some of theirs to answer your questions?
The easiest way to "think before spamming" is to structure your emails into three sections: situation, complication and solution. In the first "situation" section write a bit on the background to give your read some context. In the second "complication" section your write what your problem is. In the last section list potential solutions and ad what specific help you need from the reader. This simple structure will earn you a reputation for being "solution-oriented" rather than "problem-oriented".
Hint: How do you know if you're spamming? Check if you regularly forward emails or documents without adding more than a question along the lines of "what do I do now?" or "please advise" or "what do you think?"

* * *

239. If you can't sketch it, you aren't ready.

Einstein supposedly said, "If you can't explain it to a six-year-old, you don't understand it yourself". The same principle is also true for questions or suggestions you want to talk to colleagues about. No matter how complex your work may be, you should always be able to reduce it to a simple sketch that captures its essence.

Whether it's complex technology interfaces, cross-border processes or questions regarding marketing, sales, leadership, and culture issues – the ability to reduce things to a simple drawing is extremely important. Being able to sketch your question or suggestion shows that you've grappled with the complexities and distilled it to its core. Then, and only then, are you ready to explain it to your colleagues.

240. Share suggestions for improvement.

Sharing ideas is a numbers game. The more ideas you suggest, the likelier it is that some succeed – so don't limit yourself to your department or even geographic unit. Submitting lots of ideas will also earn you a reputation as a proactive and excellence-driven employee.

Some companies have a centralized email to which you can send such ideas. Otherwise, just send your idea(s) to the most relevant person you can find. If you don't know anyone, asking around until you find someone is a great way to grow your network within your company.

Hint: Your suggestion should always be framed positively, include a possible solution and ask for feedback. Compare "I think we could improve sales by using a green label for our salad range. What do you think?" to "Our salad packaging looks really bad – we should improve it".

Hint: A lot of "old-timers" in the office complain about the status quo but don't voice their suggestions in public. Often times, colleagues will be happy for you to submit their ideas. Just ask for permission first.

Hint: Focus your efforts on the people who appreciate your ideas and ask them if there is anything you can do on your end to help implement it. Once a suggestion of yours has been implemented, you automatically have a good story to tell your boss or someone skeptical of another idea of yours. "Remember that new packaging? I recommended changing it and helped Laura with the design and implementation. Sales are now higher than ever." This kind of story can be extremely valuable to your career (and salary).

241. Don't add coworkers to Facebook, Instagram etc.

It's very simple: don't add colleagues to non-professional social media platforms (i.e. everything except for LinkedIn and XING). The activities you partake in, the groups you are members of, the comments you make and posts you like – can you really be sure that none of your colleagues have differing political, religious or moral opinions? Do you really want them to know what your girlfriend looks like in a bikini? Can you really trust every single one of your friends not to make an embarrassing or offensive comment? Do you really want to be scrutinizing every single post or refrain from social media when in a bad mood or drinking? I rest my case.

242. Avoid gossip.

Keep your eyes and ears open, but keep your mouth shut. You'd be surprised at the number of times people who have badmouthed their (past) company or colleagues at parties, career fairs and other such events. You never know whether someone is related to management, well-connected in HR or active in reporting on your industry.

There are more than enough stories in each company about that one colleague who drank too much wine and said a few sentences that cost them their career.

As tempting as it may be to join in and talk badly about others, it won't get you anywhere in the long run. The person you gossiped about will eventually find out and (rightfully or wrongfully) assume you said something malicious.

From experience, people who gossip about others <u>with</u> you are also highly likely to gossip <u>about</u> you. Would you really trust such people with your secrets?

Gossiping also needlessly gives others leverage over you.

Imagine what can happen if you get a pay raise while the person you gossip with didn't – and is now resentful towards you.

Hint: This does not mean to avoid gossip. You don't want to be living in a bubble and not know about upcoming changes around you. Such changes can create valuable opportunities for you. As the saying goes, "Knowledge is power."

Hint: When others are gossiping, do your best to appear neutral. Use platitudes and defusing sentences such as "well everyone is different," "maybe they just had a bad day," or "oh I don't know that person that well, so I wouldn't know" etc. Otherwise try to shift the conversation towards resolving the issue with sentences "do they know what you think about ...," "have you talked to them about it," and "what do you think should be done?"

Hint: There are usually reasons why people act the way they do. If you have a problem with someone, talk to them directly. Openly addressing an issue doesn't mean you have to be aggressive or rude. Use questions ("What do you think about...?", "Do you know why ...?") or subjective statements ("I feel...," "My impression is...") to avoid an accusatory tone.

Hint: Don't snitch on others' gossiping. The person you told on will eventually find out that it was you who snitched on them. And you don't want to people who gossip as "enemies."

✶ ✶ ✶

243. Take a picture every day.

After a few months you will have a cool collection of pictures which you can share with your partner or children. In the best of cases, you can enter it into company-wide competitions or publish some of the better ones in your intranet. A year can go by quickly. You will be glad you kept track using over 220 pictures.

It doesn't matter whether you photograph the snow outside, the new coffee machine, your colleague, your team, the office plant blooming, the new headset, the convention hotel, the Christmas decoration or the new company logo – there are more than enough picture opportunities all around you. To spur your creativity and make the whole thing a bit more challenging, don't take the same picture twice.

✶ ✶ ✶

244. Be generous with business cards.

Hand out cards at every opportunity. Each time you give a card, succinctly summarize why. Something along the lines of "If you ever want to talk about truck leasing I can help you out" or "I think we could really do something about those insurance costs you mentioned, give me a call this week" or "If you know a data scientist interested in joining our team, send me an email." It may sound cheesy, but it's much better than the boring "here is my card."

Hint: When receiving business cards, use the back of the card to write down some notes regarding the person who gave you their card. These notes could be when and where you met them, what their relationship to you is as well as some personal information like their birthday or how many children they have. That way, even if you contact that person years later, you still have a bit more background information than just their company name and title.

245. Make your business card stand out.

After a while, everyone ends up with a large collection of nondescript business cards. You can make your card stand out by making it non-white (99% are white), non-standard size (99% are 85mm wide by 55mm high) or choosing a material other than paper (plastic or metal). Even if you are part of a larger company with highly standardized business card designs, you can always suggest improvements. For ideas, you can always Google "creative business cards + [your industry]" and look at the image search results.

246. Set reminders at irregular times.

If you need to remember an appointment or meeting, it is better to set an Outlook or reminder on your smartphone at 10:44

instead of 10:45. Psychologically, your brain remembers these irregular times better – try it and see.

LEAVING YOUR JOB

Switching jobs or employers multiple times during your career is the new normal. The hacks listed below help you prepare your next career move and make the change as smoothly as possible. Always leave on amicable terms so that you can return if your new job isn't what you expected it to be!

247. Keep a "master CV."

Keep a long version of your CV where you periodically add major projects and achievements. When you do leave your job, you don't have to spend hours thinking about what you did over the past years. Delete all the non-relevant parts from this "master CV" to quickly create a tailored CV.

248. Use your job before you leave it.

Before quitting, use company time and resources to maximize your market value or prepare for a successful start at your new job. Sign up for all trainings and take on assignments related to your new job. Try to visit customers or trade fairs related to your new field of employment.

You can also research potential employers or write your application papers while still at work. Beware that some companies have software monitoring your computer usage. In that case, you can just use a good old-fashioned pen and paper. You can get disciplined or even fired for stealing company time and resources, so do this at your own risk.

Hint: Don't tell anyone you're leaving for a new job until the last possible moment and only until you've signed the new employment contract. Once your boss knows you're leaving, they will minimize all expenditures related to you. That means an immediate reduction in trainings, business travel and all other perks. It can also mean being assigned all the boring work no one else wants to do (e.g. sorting five years of invoices alphabetically).

★ ★ ★

249. Never burn bridges.

As tempting as it may be to shout expletives while throwing over furniture on your last day, don't do it.

Burning the proverbial bridges can have a real impact your future success. If an ex-colleague attends the same social or business event, your night may not be a lot of fun. Equally, your new boss could be friends or neighbors with an ex-colleague of yours. Both scenarios are highly likely if you switch employers within the same industry.

Instead, take the time to thank and say goodbye to the most important people you're leaving. Thank them for their leadership, time, work, trust or friendship. That way, ex-colleagues may be more likely to forward you an interesting sales leads or share industry developments with you. Additionally, your old employer may suddenly become very successful and be offering good money to win back ex-employees.

Hint: If asked for your reasons for leaving, keep them positive or at least neutral. Acceptable reasons are better career chances, higher salaries or lower commuting times.

Hint: Offering constructive feedback as to the real reasons why you quit can backfire. However euphemistically you try to say that the hours were too long, the payment lousy or your boss just too much of a micromanager – it may be taken personally.

250. Take your important contacts with you.

If you decide to switch companies, copy the contact details of relevant people to your private directory before starting your new job. Limit yourself to people who will continue being relevant in your new role – copying the entire company directory will get you in trouble with HR (or even have legal consequences).

251. Try to influence your letter of recommendation.

A good letter of recommendation can translate into a higher salary or better position at your next job. Try to influence it as much as you can:

- Ask for your letter of recommendation at least a month before leaving your job, while your boss still has a good memory of what your responsibilities and strengths were. The fact that you are still working for your boss is also leverage – your boss knows that if they write a negative letter, then your remaining work days will probably not be very productive.

- Send your boss a suggestion of which of your responsibilities and strengths you would like included in your letter of recommendation. Be sure to include things relevant to your next job or your long-term career. Most bosses will recycle at least a part of it in order to save time.

- Schedule a meeting with your boss called "Review letter of recommendation" and ask to go through the letter together with them. Having your boss sit across from you will reduce the chances that they will write negative things about you.

- Ask for corrections if you think your letter is missing something. Your letter of recommendation is permanent – your boss will soon forget about any changes you requested. Google "best reference letter phrases" to see if your reference letter can be improved upon.

252. Write a good farewell email.

Take the time to personally say goodbye to important colleagues and friends – for the rest of the company, a farewell email suffices. Here are some dos & don'ts:

- **Write one**. Don't go quietly into the night – you want people to know you are gone. A farewell message is also a good opportunity for colleagues you haven't seen in a long time to reconnect with you.

- **Don't "send to all"**. If you work in a company bigger than 200 people, chances are about half of your recipients will not know who you are and why you are writing them. If you are leaving a large company, narrow down your recipients by geography or department.

- **Send it to your personal email.** Put everyone else on BCC. This reminds your recipients of your contact details and spares you the drama of colleagues analyzing who you sent (and didn't send) your email to.

- **Keep it short**. 2-3 short paragraphs are more than enough. The longer you've been at the company, the longer your farewell email.

- **Stay positive and be thankful**. Highlight what made your job fun and your company special. Thank your colleagues for your time together and mention what you'll miss. Wish the recipients and the company all the best.

- **Stay professional**. Even though "hasta la vista baby!" may sound tempting, you want to strike a professional tone. Don't get too emotional. Don't fill your email with #unnecessary #Hashtags. Don't include individualized shoutouts to your fifteen work buddies. A farewell email is not a high school yearbook.

- **Include your contact details**. This is important for future networking. You never know what role one of your email recipients may play at your next job (future customer, colleague, vendor etc.).

- **Spellcheck**. Enough said. Do you really want the last thing people remember about you to be that you can't differentiate between "there" and "their"?

- **Include a picture**. If you have a memorable (professional!) picture, this can make your farewell-email stand out a bit more. Examples of good pictures would be you with your team, you using a product of the company or a photo of you in your free time (e.g. with family).

- **Send it in the morning**. Send your "today is my last day" email first thing in the morning. If you send it right before you turn in your badge, you will miss out on the sudden barrage of calls, IMs and emails from colleagues who want to say their goodbyes. Block some time on your last day for replying to this sudden barrage.

- **Send personalized emails to your most important colleagues**. A personal farewell email thanking your boss or your closest coworkers really makes a difference. You can only say goodbye once, so do it right and show your appreciation to the people that made a difference.

- **Send separate emails to external contacts**. Send a more formal email to customers, vendors or business partners. These contacts may still be valuable for your next job and you want them to know where they can reach you.

253. Always talk well about your past company or colleagues.

Find the positive aspects about your past company and colleagues and talk about them. Aim for something "I previously worked for the startup SeniorCare. We managed to serve thousands of meals to senior citizens at an extremely low cost by buying surplus ingredients and adapting our menus correspondingly. I was in charge of managing relationships with wholesale food suppliers, supermarkets and retirement homes all across the US." Doesn't that sound good and make you seem like a valuable, highly skilled employee? Who cares if the SeniorCare startup failed because the IT-setup was disastrous or that you were the only one with an IQ above room temperature? Find the positives!

Hint: Badmouthing your past workplace makes no sense in a free-market economy where you can choose your employment. If your workplace was that bad, why did you (as a free person) make such a bad decision and work there?

ABOUT THE AUTHOR

Office work can be hard, confusing and frustrating. When I started out, there was no book on "office hacks." That is what motivated to me write this book. I want to help others better navigate the corporate world in order to make your life easier than mine has been.

I use a lot of these hacks on a daily basis to save time and positively influence my career. That is why I had to publish this book under a pseudonym. I don't want my colleagues or customers to constantly be second-guessing whether I am regularly hacking my workday.

To create this book, I asked a lot of senior (and junior!) employees for their advice. To give you an idea of how valuable the insights contained in this book are, I have included a brief overview of my experiences with offices and corporate life:

- Global investment bank
- Private equity firm
- Global law firm
- European consulting company for financial services
- Global consulting firm for strategy & digitalization
- European private bank
- Mentoring and work on several startups

If you enjoyed this book, please take 1-2 minutes to review it so that others can benefit from it as well.

I wish you all the best in your career and look forward to hearing from you! Write to me at james.o.king@outlook.com or visit www.winnerhacks.com

COPYRIGHT

© 2020 M.S.R.L. Graebner

All rights reserved.

No part of this book may be reproduced, or stored in a retrieval system, or transmitted in any form or by any means, electronic, mechanical, photocopying, recording, or otherwise, without express written permission of the publisher.

The characters and events portrayed in this book are fictitious. Any similarity to real persons, living or dead, is coincidental and not intended by the author.

Cover design by: M.S.R.L. Graebner
(based on an pxhere-image from Mohamed Hassan; reprinted with permission)

First Edition

www.ingramcontent.com/pod-product-compliance
Lightning Source LLC
Chambersburg PA
CBHW020655220526
45464CB00001B/447